501 Civil War Quotes and Notes

Learn Civil War History From The Words Of Those Who Lived It And Made It

Features quotes made before, during, and after the Civil War. Learn about the military commanders, political leaders, battles, places, soldiers, abolitionists, and the people of Civil War times. Each quote has an informative note.

Edited By Jonathan R. Allen

Learn more about the
Civil War at my website:
LearnCivilWarHistory.com

Follow me on Twitter and
learn Civil War history
from my Tweets:
@CivilWarHistory

Cover Image: Battle of the Wilderness
Desperate fight on the Orange Court
House Plank Road, near Todd's Tavern,
May 6th, 1864, by Kurz & Allison

Warranty Notice

The Publisher has striven to be as accurate and complete as possible in the creation of this book, notwithstanding the fact that he does not warrant or represent at any time that the contents within are accurate due to the changing nature of the study and research of the history of the Civil War. While all attempts have been made to verify information provided in this publication, the Publisher assumes no responsibility for errors, omissions, or contrary interpretation of the subject matter herein. Any perceived slights of specific persons, peoples, or organizations are unintentional. In practical advice books or educational books, like anything else in life, there are no guarantees of income made or improvement of skill. Readers are cautioned to rely on their own judgment about their individual circumstances to act accordingly. This book and the content provided herein are simply for educational purposes. Every effort has been made to ensure that the content provided in this book is accurate and helpful for its readers at publishing time. However, this is not an exhaustive treatment of the subjects. No liability is assumed for losses or damages due to the information provided. You are responsible for your own choices, actions, and results. You should consult your attorney for your specific publishing and disclaimer questions and needs.

Copyright Notice

Contents

How This Book Will Help You
To Learn About The Civil War

For both the new recruit and for the veteran Civil War student, there is an opportunity here in these 501 quotes and notes to learn about the Civil War. The presentation is simple, I give you a Civil War quote and then in an informative note I provide a brief background regarding some of the circumstances of the quote.

This book has 501 quotes, but it is a mere drop in the ocean of Civil War quotes. These quotes and their notes are not an exhaustive study of the Civil War. I read once that it is estimated that over 65,000 books have been written about the Civil War. Imagine how many quotes there are from the Civil War! An immeasurable amount, I think. Although these quotes and notes in this book are accurate and self-standing, I strove, for the most part, to keep them brief. In many, if not all, cases there is much more that could be written for a particular quote and its note. The quotes often times have many additional words or text which were spoken or written before or after the quoted text I used in this book. Sometimes pages and pages of additional words, if not an entire book, could be written as a note to explain some of the quotes. In both the quotes and the notes, my goal was for accuracy and brevity without losing completeness and value.

The quotes or notes may make you stop and think. Perhaps a quote or a note will have you wondering about how uncomfortable and hard it must have been to be a Civil War soldier on a long march in rain and cold. Reading other quotes and notes might have you imagine what it was like to be in a Civil War battle. You may gain some insight into the character and personality of some Civil War leaders and commanders by reading their quotes and notes. Some quotes and notes may make you sad as the Civil War was a time of great bloodshed and loss. I hope some quotes and notes make you chuckle. The people of Civil War times were real people living through hell on Earth, but they sometimes found relief with humor.

The quotes and notes are numbered but not chronological, nor are they organized by subject or topic matter. You may read the quotes and notes from first to last, or you may randomly thumb-through the book. Sometimes there will be a sequence of quotes and notes which are related. Sometimes the quotes and notes will be unrelated to one another. You might best enjoy reading the quotes and notes by casually paging through and skipping around as you please, reading whichever ones happen to catch your attention and fancy at the moment.

Although I have occasionally added brackets containing needed clarifying words to some quotes, I made no grammar, spelling, or punctuation corrections to the quotes. The quotes in this book are as they were originally written or spoken. You will see that some quotes have words which are spelled phonetically. Some of those who are quoted were good writers or speakers with good educations. Others who are quoted were not perhaps the best writers or speakers and their educations were not complete, but they did communicate successfully with their words.

I hope that some of the quotes and notes spur you on to learn more about the Civil War. Perhaps a quote or a note about a certain battle, person, or place, will kick-start your curiosity and desire to learn more. You may go on to become an expert on the Civil War, or maybe take a special interest in a particular Civil War topic. A whole new world of Civil War learning might open for you by the spark of curiosity brought on by a quote or a note in this book. That would be a good thing because there is so much to learn about the Civil War.

There's always more and more to learn about the Civil War. Learning about the Civil War can be an enjoyable and rewarding endeavor that will last throughout your lifetime. I urge you to read about the Civil War and to visit battlefield parks. Enjoy and have fun learning about the Civil War. May your Civil War learning journey start or continue here.

Quotes About History

"The histories of the Lost Cause are all written out by big bugs, generals and reknowned historians. Well, I had as much right as any man to write a history."
* Sam Watkins (1839-1901), of Company H, 1st Tennessee of Nashville. Author of: *Co. Aytch: A Side Show of the Big Show.*

"History must stay open, it is all humanity."
* William Carlos Williams (1883-1963), American author and poet.

"Those who cannot remember the past are condemned to repeat it."
* George Santayana (1863-1952), philosopher and poet.

"The past is never dead. It's not even past."
* William Faulkner

"History is not was, it is."
* William Faulkner

501 Civil War Quotes and Notes

#1. "That this nation, under God, shall have a new birth of freedom, and that government of the people, by the people, for the people, shall not perish from the earth."
* President Abraham Lincoln, from his Gettysburg Address given at Gettysburg, Pennsylvania on November 19, 1863.

#2. "Neither let us be slandered from our duty by false accusations against us, nor frightened from it by menaces of destruction to the Government nor of dungeons to ourselves. Let us have faith that right makes might, and in that faith, let us, to the end, dare to do our duty as we understand it."
* Abraham Lincoln, from his Cooper Institute (Cooper Union) address made in New York City to members of the Young Men's Republican Union on February 27, 1860. This address gave a strong moral argument for ending the spread of slavery into the territories.

#3. "Fellow-citizens, we cannot escape history. We of this Congress and this administration, will be remembered in spite of ourselves. No personal significance, or insignificance, can spare one or another of us. The fiery trial through which we pass, will light us down, in honor or dishonor, to the latest generation. We say we are for the Union. The world will not forget that we say this. We know how to save the Union. The world knows we do know how to save it. We — even we here — hold the power, and bear the responsibility. In giving freedom to the slave, we assure freedom to the free — honorable alike in what we give, and what we preserve. We shall nobly save, or meanly lose, the last best hope of earth. Other means may succeed; this could not fail. The way is plain, peaceful, generous, just — a way which, if followed, the world will forever applaud, and God must forever bless."
* President Abraham Lincoln, from his Second Annual Message to Congress given on December 1, 1862. This was one month before he issued his Emancipation Proclamation.

#4. "A house divided against itself cannot stand. I believe this government cannot endure, permanently, half slave and half free. I do not expect the Union to be dissolved — I do not expect the house to fall — but I do expect it will cease to be divided. It will become all one thing or all the other. Either the opponents of slavery will arrest the further spread of it, and place it where the public mind shall rest in the belief that it is in the course of ultimate extinction; or its advocates will push it forward, till it shall become lawful in all the States, old as well as new — North as well as South."
* Abraham Lincoln, from his prophetic House Divided speech made on June 16, 1858, at the Illinois State Capital in Springfield. Lincoln was accepting the Illinois Republican Party's nomination for United States senator. He would lose to Stephen A. Douglas, but their contest for office would be highlighted by their famous Lincoln-Douglas Debates.

#5. "With malice toward none; with charity for all; with firmness in the right, as God gives us to see the right, let us strive on to finish the work we are in; to bind up the nation's wounds; to care for him who shall have borne the battle, and for his widow, and his orphan--to do all which may achieve and cherish a just and lasting peace, among ourselves, and with all nations."
* From President Abraham Lincoln's Second Inaugural Address, March 4, 1865. Lincoln's Second Inaugural Address is one of the most highly regarded speeches ever made in United States history.

#6. "I have heard something said on this and a former occasion about allegiance to the South. I know no South, no North, no East, no West, to which I owe any allegiance. I owe allegiance to two sovereignty, and only two: one is the sovereignty of this Union, and the other is the sovereignty of the state of Kentucky. My allegiance is to this Union and to my state; but if gentlemen suppose they can exact from me an acknowledgment of allegiance to any ideal or future contemplated confederacy of the South, I here declare that I owe no allegiance to it; nor will I, for one, come under any such allegiance if I can avoid it."
* From a 1848 Senate speech by Kentucky Senator Henry Clay. Mississippi Senator Henry Foote had questioned Clay regarding his allegiance to the South. Clay makes it plain in this quote where his allegiance is, which is to the Union and to Kentucky. Henry Clay was known as "The Great Compromiser" or "The Great Pacifier" due to his ability to achieve

agreement between differing groups. This quote is indicative of the growing tensions between the states before the Civil War.

#7. "No other terms than unconditional and immediate surrender. I propose to move immediately upon your works."
* General Ulysses S. Grant to Confederate General Simon Bolivar Buckner, at Fort Donelson on February 16, 1862. It's from this quote and a play on his initials, that U. S. Grant gained the nickname of "Unconditional Surrender" Grant.

#8. "I propose to fight it out on this line, if it takes all summer."
* General Ulysses S. Grant showing his bulldog attitude in a dispatch to Washington made on May 11, 1864, before Spotsylvania Court House.

#9. "Let us have peace."
* Ulysses S. Grant, while accepting the nomination for president on May 29, 1868.

#10. "John Brown's effort was peculiar. It was not a slave insurrection. It was an attempt by white men to get up a revolt among slaves, in which the slaves refused to participate."
* Abraham Lincoln on February 27, 1860, in his Cooper Union Address. Abolitionist John Brown made his raid on Harpers Ferry during October 16-18, 1859. Brown's raid was a failure and he was executed on December 2, 1859.

#11. "Plainly, the central idea of secession, is the essence of anarchy."
* From President Abraham Lincoln's First Inaugural Address made on March 4, 1861.

#12. "The Constitution, in all its provisions, looks to an indestructible Union, composed of indestructible states."
* Salmon P. Chase, in a 1869 Supreme Court opinion.

#13. "One flag, one land, one heart, one hand, One Nation, evermore!"
* Oliver Wendell Holmes, Sr., in 1862, stating his support for the Union. Holmes was a doctor, poet, and pundit. He was regarded as one of the top writers of the 1800s. His son, Oliver Wendell Holmes Jr., fought for the Union in the Civil War and later became a member of the Supreme Court.

#14. "All the armies of Europe, Asia, and Africa combined, with all the treasure of the earth (our own excepted) in their military chest, with a Bonaparte for a commander, could not, by force, take a drink from the Ohio, or make a track on the Blue Ridge, in a trial of a thousand years."
* Abraham Lincoln, from a speech given on January 27, 1838, to the Springfield, Illinois Young Men's Lyceum.

#15. "At what point, then, is the approach of danger to be expected? I answer, if it ever reach us, it must spring up amongst us; it cannot come from abroad. If destruction be our lot, we must ourselves be its author and finisher. As a nation of freemen, we must live through all time, or die by suicide."
* Abraham Lincoln, from a speech given on January 27, 1838, to the Springfield, Illinois Young Men's Lyceum. Here, a young Abraham Lincoln seems to be foretelling the Civil War.

#16. "No man can put a chain about the ankle of his fellow man without at last finding the other end fastened around his own neck."
* From a 1883 speech given by abolitionist Frederick Douglass.

#17. "The fight must go on. The cause of civil liberty must not be surrendered at the end of one or even one hundred defeats."
* Abraham Lincoln, from a letter written to Henry Ashbury, 1858.

#18. "I, Robert E. Lee of Lexington, Virginia do solemn, in the presence of Almighty God, that I will henceforth faithfully support, protect and defend the Constitution of the United States, the Union of the States thereafter, and that I will, in like manner, abide by and faithful support all laws and

proclamations which have been made during the existing rebellion with reference to the emancipation of slaves, so help me God."
* Former Confederate General Robert E. Lee's amnesty oath to the United States, October 2, 1865.

#19. "See! There is Jackson standing like a stone wall."
* Bernard Bee at First Bull Run, July 21, 1861, thus leading Confederate Thomas Jonathan Jackson to be called "Stonewall Jackson." Although it is accepted that Bee was rallying troops with his words, and was praising Jackson for holding his ground, there is some debate as to what exactly Bee meant. Some believe Bee was expressing his unhappiness with Jackson for staying put during the battle, and for not changing position as circumstances may have required. It is a topic of Civil War debate. It became impossible to ask Bee to explain exactly what he meant, Bee was killed at First Bull Run.

#20. "All quiet along the Potomac," 'they said,' "Except, now and then a stray picket Is shot as he walks on his beat to and fro By a rifleman hid in the thicket."
* From Ethel Lynn Beers' "The Picket Guard," as printed in *Harper's Weekly*. September 30, 1861.

#21. "Universal suffrage, furloughs, and whiskey have ruined us."
* Confederate General Braxton Bragg after the Battle of Shiloh, fought April 6-7, 1862.

#22. "I am exceedingly anxious that this Union, the Constitution, and the liberties of the people shall be perpetuated in accordance with the original idea for which that struggle was made, and I shall be most happy indeed if I shall be an humble instrument in the hands of the Almighty, and of this, his almost chosen people, for perpetuating the object of that great struggle."
* Abraham Lincoln speaking to the New Jersey Senate on February 21, 1861. His inauguration would be on March 4.

#23. "Since Vicksburg they have not had a word to say against Grant's habits. He has the disagreeable habit of not retreating before irresistible veterans."
* Mary Chesnut's husband, James Chesnut, was a South Carolina United States senator. When South Carolina seceded, he resigned and became a brigadier general in the Confederate Army. Mary Chesnut kept a diary during the Civil War, this is her January 1, 1864, diary entry.

#24. "We feel that our cause is just and holy; we protest solemnly in the face of mankind that we desire peace at any sacrifice save that of honor and independence; we seek no conquest, no aggrandizement, no concession of any kind from the States with which we were lately confederated; all we ask is to be let alone; that those who never held power over us shall not now attempt our subjugation by arms. This we will, this we must, resist to the direst extremity. The moment that this pretension is abandoned the sword will drop from our grasp, and we shall be ready to enter into treaties of amity and commerce that cannot but be mutually beneficial. So long as this pretension is maintained, with a firm reliance on that Divine Power which covers with its protection the just cause, we will continue to struggle for our inherent right to freedom, independence, and self-government."
* Confederate President Jefferson Davis on April 29, 1861, to the Confederate Congress meeting in Montgomery, Alabama. This speech would be known as Davis' "all we ask is to be let alone" speech.

#25. "Damn the torpedoes - full speed ahead!"
* Admiral David Farragut, at the Battle of Mobile Bay, on August 5, 1864. A torpedo during the Civil War was a mine that exploded upon contact. It would float on the water's surface, or submerged slightly below it.

#26. "The rebels now have in their ranks their last man. The little boys and old men are guarding prisoners and railroad bridges, and forming a good part of their forces, manning forts and positions, and any man lost by them cannot be replaced. They have robbed the cradle and the grave."
* General Ulysses S. Grant, from a published letter of August 16, 1864.

#27. "The war is over - the rebels are our countrymen again."

* General Ulysses S. Grant asking Union forces not to cheer after General Robert E. Lee surrendered at Appomattox Court House, Virginia, on April 9, 1865.

#28.
Mine eyes have seen the glory of the coming of the Lord,
He is trampling out the vintage where the grapes of wrath are stored
He hath loosed the fateful lightning of His terrible swift sword,
His truth is marching on.

Chorus: Glory, Glory, hallelujah!
Glory, glory, hallelujah!
Glory, glory, hallelujah!
His truth is marching on.

I have seen Him in the watch-fires of a hundred circling camps,
They have builded Him an altar in the evening dews and damps.
I can read His righteous sentence by the dim and flaring lamps;
His day is marching on.

(Chorus)

I have read a fiery gospel writ in burnished rows of steel
As ye deal with my condemners,
So with you my grace shall deal;
Let the Hero, born of woman,
Crush the serpent with his heel;
Since God is marching on.

(Chorus)

He has sounded forth the trumpet that shall never call retreat;
He is sifting out the hearts of men before his Judgment Seat.
Oh! Be swift, my soul, to answer him, be jubilant, my feet!
Our God is marching on.

(Chorus)

In the beauty of the lilies Christ was born across the sea

With a glory in his bosom
That transfigures you and me;
As he died to make men holy let us die to make men free,
While God is marching on.

(Chorus)
* The lyrics from Julia Ward Howe's first published version of the "Battle Hymn of the Republic." The song uses the music of the song "John Brown's Body." Howe wrote the song in November 1861, and it was first published in *The Atlantic Monthly* in February 1862.

#29. "I can anticipate no greater calamity for the country than a dissolution of the Union. It would be an accumulation of all the evils we complain of, and I am willing to sacrifice anything but honor for its preservation."
* Robert E. Lee, from a letter of January 23, 1861. Despite these words from Robert E. Lee, his military leadership in the Civil War was not performed in the interest of preserving the Union.

#30. "If the Union is dissolved, and the government disrupted, I shall return to my native state and share the miseries of my people, and save in defense will draw my sword no more."
* Robert E. Lee, from a letter of January 23, 1861. Lee chose to draw his sword, he would lead the Army of Northern Virginia in the Civil War. Lee would take the Army of Northern Virginia on two offensive invasions into the North, first at Antietam in 1862, and then Gettysburg in 1863.

#31. "Never mind, General, all this has been my fault; it is I that have lost this fight, and you must help me out of it in the best way you can."
* General Robert E. Lee, to General Wilcox after the failure of Pickett's Charge at the Battle of Gettysburg on July 3, 1863. Colonel A. J. Lyon Fremantle of the British Army was with Lee and an observer. Fremantle included this Lee quote in his diary.

#32. "This has been a sad day for us, Colonel, a sad day; but we can't always expect to gain victories."

* General Robert E. Lee to Colonel A. J. Lyon Fremantle of the British Army after the failure of Pickett's Charge at the Battle of Gettysburg on July 3, 1863.

#33. "I have been up to see the Congress and they do not seem to be able to do anything except to eat peanuts and chew tobacco, while my army is starving."
* General Robert E. Lee, March 1865. The Civil War had taken a toll on Lee's Army of Northern Virginia and the once powerful army was now on its last legs. Supplies were scarce and Lee asked the Confederate Congress for help, this quote shows his frustration. Lee would surrender to Ulysses S. Grant at Appomattox Court House on April 9.

#34. "We failed, but in the good providence of God apparent failure often proves a blessing."
* Robert E. Lee, from a letter of March 22, 1869.

#35. "If we do not make common cause to save the good old ship of the Union on this voyage, nobody will have a chance to pilot her on another voyage."
* Abraham Lincoln, from a speech made in Cleveland, Ohio on February 15, 1861. Abraham Lincoln came to Cleveland only twice, once in life and once in death. This quote is from a speech he made while traveling from Springfield, Illinois to Washington D. C. for his inauguration. In death, Abraham Lincoln would return to Cleveland when his funeral train arrived there in April 1865. Lincoln's casket was taken by horse and carriage to Monument Park (now known as Public Square) where thousands viewed his open casket.

#36. "In your hands my dissatisfied fellow-country-men, and not in mine, is the momentous issue of civil war. The government will not assail you."
* An excerpt from President Abraham Lincoln's first inaugural address given on March 4, 1861. Lincoln's words here are directed to the South. The Southern states began to secede from the Union soon after Lincoln was elected president. The Southern states seceded in a pattern of two waves.

Order and Dates Of Secession of the Confederate States:

The First Wave – The Lower South
1. South Carolina – December 20, 1860
2. Mississippi – January 9, 1861
3. Florida – January 10, 1861
4. Alabama – January 11, 1861
5. Georgia – January 19, 1861
6. Louisiana – January 26, 1861
7. Texas – February 1, 1861

The Second Wave – The Upper South
8. Virginia – April 17, 1861
9. Arkansas – May 6, 1861
10. North Carolina – May 20, 1861
11. Tennessee – June 8, 1861

#37. "My paramount object in this struggle is to save the Union, and is not either to save or destroy slavery. If I could save the Union without freeing any slave, I would do it; and if could save it by freeing all the slaves, I would do it; and if I could save it by freeing some and leaving the others alone, I would also do that."
* President Abraham Lincoln, in a letter to Horace Greeley, August 22, 1862. Greeley was the founder and editor of the *New-York Tribune*. Note that at this time Lincoln had written the Emancipation Proclamation, but had not yet released it.

#38. "I intend no modification of my oft-expressed personal wish that all men everywhere could be free."
* President Abraham Lincoln, in a letter to Horace Greeley of the *New-York Tribune*. August 22, 1862.

#39. "I would rather have the applause of a Negro to that of the president!"
* President Abraham Lincoln saw John Wilkes Booth act in plays at Ford's Theater. The president enjoyed Booth's acting talents and he was in attendance for the play *Marble Heart* at Ford's Theater on November 9, 1863, in which Booth performed and won good reviews. After the play,

Lincoln sent a note to the actor inviting him to the White House so they could meet. Booth did not take Lincoln up on the offer to meet and this was his remark to a friend. John Wilkes Booth, the actor turned assassin, shot President Abraham Lincoln at Ford's Theater the evening of April 14, 1865. Lincoln died early in the morning of April 15.

#40.
Executive Mansion
Washington, January 26, 1863

Major General Hooker:
General.

I have placed you at the head of the Army of the Potomac. Of course I have done this upon what appear to me to be sufficient reasons. And yet I think it best for you to know that there are some things in regard to which, I am not quite satisfied with you. I believe you to be a brave and a skilful soldier, which, of course, I like. I also believe you do not mix politics with your profession, in which you are right. You have confidence in yourself, which is a valuable, if not an indispensable quality. You are ambitious, which, within reasonable bounds, does good rather than harm. But I think that during Gen. Burnside's command of the Army, you have taken counsel of your ambition, and thwarted him as much as you could, in which you did a great wrong to the country, and to a most meritorious and honorable brother officer. I have heard, in such way as to believe it, of your recently saying that both the Army and the Government needed a Dictator. Of course it was not for this, but in spite of it, that I have given you the command. Only those generals who gain successes, can set up dictators. What I now ask of you is military success, and I will risk the dictatorship. The government will support you to the utmost of it's ability, which is neither more nor less than it has done and will do for all commanders. I much fear that the spirit which you have aided to infuse into the Army, of criticising their Commander, and withholding confidence from him, will now turn upon you. I shall assist you as far as I can, to put it down. Neither you, nor Napoleon, if he were alive again, could get any good out of an army, while such a spirit prevails in it.

And now, beware of rashness. Beware of rashness, but with energy, and sleepless vigilance, go forward, and give us victories.

Yours very truly
A. Lincoln
* This is a January 26, 1863, letter from President Abraham Lincoln to
General Joseph "Fighting Joe" Hooker. President Abraham Lincoln
appointed Hooker as commander of the Army of the Potomac on January
25, 1863. Lincoln was looking for a commander who would bring the Union
victories on the battlefields, so far, he had not found that commander. Now,
it was Hooker who would have his chance to lead the Army of the Potomac,
but he would lose to Robert E. Lee at Chancellorsville. Before the Battle of
Gettysburg in early July 1863, Lincoln would replace "Fighting Joe" Hooker
with George G. Meade as the commander of the Army of the Potomac.
"Fighting Joe" would not have the opportunity to set up a dictatorship, and
Meade would defeat Lee at Gettysburg.

#41. "I should like to know, if taking this old Declaration of Independence,
which declares that all men are equal upon principle, and making
exceptions to it, where will it stop? If one man says it does not mean a
negro, why may not another man say it does not mean another man? If the
Declaration is not the truth, let us get the statute book in which we find it
and tear it out. Who is so bold as to do it? If it is not true, let us tear it out."
* Abraham Lincoln during the Lincoln-Douglas Debates, 1858.

#42. "When Grant once gets possession of a place, he holds on to it as if he
had inherited it."
* President Abraham Lincoln. June 22, 1864.

#43. "With malice toward none, with charity for all, with firmness in the
right, as God gives us to see the right, let us strive on to finish the work we
are in, to bind up the nation's wounds, to care for him who shall have borne
the battle, and for his widow and his orphan, to do all which may achieve
and cherish a just and lasting peace among ourselves, and with all nations."
* President Abraham Lincoln, from his second inaugural address. March 4,
1865.

#44. "Enough lives have been sacrificed. We must extinguish our resentments if we expect harmony and union."
* President Abraham Lincoln, speaking to his Cabinet on April 14, 1865. Only hours later he would be felled by an assassin's bullet at Ford's Theater.

#45.
"All quiet along the Potomac," they say,
Except now and then a stray picket
Is shot as he walks on his beat to and fro,
By a rifleman hid in the thicket.
'Tis nothing. A private or two now and then
Will not count in the news of the battle;
Not an officer lost. Only one of the men
Moaning out all alone the death rattle.
All quiet along the Potomac tonight,
Where the soldiers lie peacefully dreaming,
Their tents in the rays of the clear autumn moon,
O'er the light of the watch fires, are gleaming;
There's only the sound of the lone sentry's tread
As he tramps from the rock to the fountain,
And thinks of the two in the low trundle bed,
Far away in the cot on the mountain.

His musket falls slack, and his face, dark and grim,
Grows gentle with memories tender,
As he mutters a prayer for the children asleep,
For their mother, may Heaven defend her.
The moon seems to shine just as brightly as then
That night when the love yet unspoken
Leaped up to his lips when low-murmured vows
Were pledged to be ever unbroken.

Then drawing his sleeve roughly over his eyes,
He dashes off tears that are welling,
And gathers his gun closer up to its place
As if to keep down the heart-swelling.
He passes the fountain, the blasted pine tree,
The footstep is lagging and weary;

Yet onward he goes, through the broad belt of light,
Toward the shades of the forest so dreary.

Hark! Was it the night wind that rustled the leaves?
Was it moonlight so wondrously flashing?
It looks like a rifle -- "Ah! Mary, good-bye!"
And the lifeblood is ebbing and splashing.
All quiet along the Potomac tonight,
No sound save the rush of the river;
While soft falls the dew on the face of the dead --
The picket's off duty forever.
* The lyrics of the popular Civil War song "All Quiet Along the Potomac Tonight."

#46. "Up, men, and to your posts! Don't forget today that you are from Old Virginia!"
* General George E. Pickett to his men before Pickett's Charge (also known as the Pickett-Pettigrew assault/charge or Longstreet's assault/charge) made on the Union center on Cemetery Ridge at the Battle of Gettysburg on July 3, 1863. Confederate casualties were high, many of Pickett's men never returned to "Old Virginia" with life in their bodies.

#47. "I begin to regard the death and mangling of a couple thousand men as a small affair, a kind of morning dash-and it may be well that we become so hardened."
* General William Tecumseh Sherman in a letter to his wife, July 1864. William and Ellen Ewing Sherman had eight children. Two of them died during the Civil War.

#48. "In revolution men fall and rise. Long before this war is over, much as you hear me praised now, you may hear me cursed and insulted."
* General William Tecumseh Sherman in a letter to his wife Ellen, 1864.

William Tecumseh Sherman

#49. "If the people raise a great howl against my barbarity and cruelty, I will answer that war is war, and not a popularity seeking. If they want peace, they and their relatives must stop the war."
* General William Tecumseh Sherman, from a letter to General Halleck before Sherman's march through Georgia. September 4, 1864.

#50. "Until we can repopulate Georgia, it is useless for us to occupy it; but the utter destruction of its roads, houses and people will cripple their military resources. I can make this march, and make Georgia howl."
* General William T. Sherman, from a telegram sent to General Ulysses S. Grant. Atlanta, Georgia. September 9, 1864.

#51. "Sir: The fortune of war has placed Atlanta in your hands. As mayor of the city I ask protection of non-combatants and private property."
* Mayor James Calhoun of Atlanta, Georgia, writing to Union General William Tecumseh Sherman upon surrendering the city to Sherman on September 2, 1864. Sherman responded to Calhoun by ordering that those citizens remaining in Atlanta should evacuate. Mayor Calhoun and the Atlanta city council then protested, saying those citizens of the city who remain are unable to evacuate because they are aged, sick, pregnant, or poor. General Sherman's response to this may be read in the following quote:

#52. "Gentleman: I have your letter of the 11th, in the nature of a petition to revoke my orders removing all the inhabitants from Atlanta. I have read it carefully, and give full credit to your statements of distress that will be occasioned, and yet shall not revoke my orders, because they were not designed to meet the humanities of the cause, but to prepare for the future struggles in which millions of good people outside of Atlanta have a deep interest. We must have peace, not only at Atlanta, but in all America. To secure this, we must stop the war that now desolates our once happy and favored country. To stop war, we must defeat the rebel armies which are arrayed against the laws and Constitution that all must respect and obey. To defeat those armies, we must prepare the way to reach them in their recesses, provided with the arms and instruments which enable us to accomplish our purpose. Now, I know the vindictive nature of our enemy, that we may have many years of military operations from this quarter; and, therefore, deem it wise and prudent to prepare in time. The use of Atlanta for warlike purposes in inconsistent with its character as a home for families. There will be no manufacturers, commerce, or agriculture here, for the maintenance of families, and sooner or later want will compel the inhabitants to go. Why not go now, when all the arrangements are completed for the transfer, instead of waiting till the plunging shot of contending armies will renew the scenes of the past month? Of course, I do not apprehend any such things at this moment, but you do not suppose this army will be here until the war is over. I cannot discuss this subject with you fairly, because I cannot impart to you what we propose to do, but I assert that our military plans make it necessary for the inhabitants to go away, and I can only renew my offer of services to make their exodus in any direction as easy and comfortable as possible. You cannot qualify war in harsher terms than I will.

"War is cruelty, and you cannot refine it; and those who brought war into our country deserve all the curses and maledictions a people can pour out. I know I had no hand in making this war, and I know I will make more sacrifices to-day than any of you to secure peace. But you cannot have peace and a division of our country. If the United States submits to a division now, it will not stop, but will go on until we reap the fate of Mexico, which is eternal war. The United States does and must assert its authority, wherever it once had power; for, if it relaxes one bit to pressure, it is gone, and I believe that such is the national feeling. This feeling assumes various shapes, but always comes back to that of Union. Once admit the Union, once more acknowledge the authority of the national Government, and, instead of devoting your houses and streets and roads to the dread uses of war, I and this army become at once your protectors and supporters, shielding you from danger, let it come from what quarter it may. I know that a few individuals cannot resist a torrent of error and passion, such as swept the South into rebellion, but you can point out, so that we may know those who desire a government, and those who insist on war and its desolation. You might as well appeal against the thunder-storm as against these terrible hardships of war. They are inevitable, and the only way the people of Atlanta can hope once more to live in peace and quiet at home, is to stop the war, which can only be done by admitting that it began in error and is perpetuated in pride. We don't want your Negroes, or your horses, or your lands, or any thing you have, but we do want and will have a just obedience to the laws of the United States. That we will have, and if it involved the destruction of your improvements, we cannot help it. You have heretofore read public sentiment in your newspapers, that live by falsehood and excitement; and the quicker you seek for truth in other quarters, the better. I repeat then that, by the original compact of government, the United States had certain rights in Georgia, which have never been relinquished and never will be; that the South began the war by seizing forts, arsenals, mints, custom-houses, etc., etc., long before Mr. Lincoln was installed, and before the South had one jot or title of provocation. I myself have seen in Missouri, Kentucky, Tennessee, and Mississippi, hundreds and thousands of women and children fleeing from your armies and desperadoes, hungry and with bleeding feet. In Memphis, Vicksburg, and Mississippi, we fed thousands and thousands of the families of rebel soldiers left on our hands, and whom we could not see starve. Now that war comes to you, you feel very different. You deprecate its horrors, but did not feel them when you sent car-loads of soldiers and ammunition, and moulded shells and shot, to carry war into Kentucky and Tennessee, to desolate the homes of hundreds and thousands of good people who only asked to live in peace at their old homes, and under the Government of their inheritance. But these comparisons are idle. I want peace, and believe it can only be reached through union and war, and I will ever conduct war with a view to perfect an early success. But, my dear sirs, when peace does come, you may call on me for any thing. Then will I share with you the last cracker, and watch with you to shield your homes and families against danger from every quarter. Now you must go, and take with you the old and feeble, feed and nurse them, and build for them, in more quiet places, proper habitations to shield them against the weather until the mad passions of men cool down, and allow the Union and peace once more to settle over your old homes in Atlanta.

"Yours in haste,

"W.T. Sherman, Major-General commanding"
* General William Tecumseh Sherman's "war is cruelty" letter to Atlanta Mayor James Calhoun after the mayor protested Sherman's order that Atlanta is to be completely evacuated by all of its citizens. Atlanta was held and occupied by Sherman for two months. On November 15, 1864, much of Atlanta was burned.

#53. "One eighth of the whole population were colored slaves, not distributed generally over the Union, but localized in the Southern part of

it. These slaves constituted a peculiar and powerful interest. All knew that this interest was, somehow, the cause of the war."
* President Abraham Lincoln, from his Second Inaugural Address on March 4, 1865.

#54. "It is well that War is so terrible, or we should grow too fond of it."
* General Robert E. Lee to James Longstreet at the Battle of Fredericksburg, December 13, 1862. At Fredericksburg, the slaughter was great. The Union made wave after wave after wave of failed assaults, leaving the battlefield strewn with dead and wounded soldiers in blue uniforms.

#55. "War means fighting, and fighting means killing."
* Confederate cavalry officer Nathan Bedford Forrest sums up what war is all about.

#56. "I will let him remain here for a few days but will not take him into danger."
* During General Ulysses S. Grant's Fort Donelson campaign, Grant's wife Julia sent their son Fred to Grant's headquarters so the twelve-year-old Fred could learn something of his father's military exploits. Grant did not want young Fred around the army too long, there was danger in the air and home is where Fred belonged.

#57. "People who are anxious to bring on war don't know what they are bargaining for; they don't see all the horrors that must accompany such an event."
* General Thomas Jonathan "Stonewall" Jackson.

#58. "Time sets all things right. Error lives but a day. Truth is eternal."
* General James Longstreet. James "Pete" Longstreet was one of the most prominent Confederate generals. Robert E. Lee called Longstreet his "Old War Horse."

#59. "No, you greatly overestimate my capacity for usefulness. A better man will soon be sent to take my place."
* General Thomas Jonathan "Stonewall" Jackson. Stonewall greatly underestimated his importance and usefulness to the Army of Northern Virginia.

#60. "You may be whatever you resolve to be."
* General Thomas Jonathan "Stonewall" Jackson kept a small notebook where he wrote down sayings or thoughts which he believed were good rules for personal conduct. The content of Jackson's book was published in chapter three of *Memoirs of Stonewall Jackson by His Widow Mary Anna Jackson* (1895). These statements (or maxims as they have popularly been called), were collected by Stonewall, so they are not necessarily his own words. They are quotes Jackson believed were of value to him and a guide as to how he ought to live his life.

#61. "I am naturally anti-slavery. If slavery is not wrong, nothing is wrong. I can not remember when I did not so think, and feel. And yet I have never understood that the Presidency conferred upon me an unrestricted right to act officially upon this judgment and feeling."
* From a letter President Abraham Lincoln wrote to Albert Hodges, who was the editor of the Kentucky newspaper *Frankfort Commonwealth,* April 4, 1864.

#62. "This is no ordinary war, and the brave and gallant Federal officers were the very kind that must be killed. Shoot the brave officers and the cowards will run away and take the brave men with them."
* During the Valley Campaign at The Battle of Port Republic fought on June 9, 1862, Confederate General Richard Ewell saw a Union officer on a white horse openly making himself a tempting target. The Union officer was at great risk of being shot by Ewell's men, but Ewell was so impressed by the Yankee officer's bravery, that he told his men not to shoot. Upon hearing of this incident, Ewell's commander, General Thomas Jonathan "Stonewall" Jackson, had these words of admonishment for his officers.

#63.
Longstreet: "General, do not all those multitudes of Federals frighten you?"

Jackson: "We shall see very soon whether I shall not frighten them."

Longstreet: "But, Jackson, what are you going to do with all those people over there?"

Jackson: "Sir, we shall give them the bayonet."
* An exchange between Confederate Generals James Longstreet and Thomas Jonathan "Stonewall" Jackson before Fredericksburg.

#64. "In this enlightened age, there are few I believe, but what will acknowledge, that slavery as an institution, is a moral & political evil in any Country. It is useless to expatiate on its disadvantages. I think it however a greater evil to the white man than to the black race, & while my feelings are strongly enlisted in behalf of the latter, my sympathies are more strong for the former. The blacks are immeasurably better off here than in Africa, morally, socially & physically. The painful discipline they are undergoing, is necessary for their instruction as a race, & I hope will prepare & lead them to better things. How long their subjugation may be necessary is known & ordered by a wise Merciful Providence. Their emancipation will sooner result from the mild & melting influence of Christianity, than the storms & tempests of fiery Controversy. This influence though slow, is sure. The doctrines & miracles of our Saviour have required nearly two thousand years, to Convert but a small part of the human race, & even among Christian nations, what gross errors still exist! While we see the Course of the final abolition of human Slavery is onward, & we give it the aid of our prayers & all justifiable means in our power, we must leave the progress as well as the result in his hands who sees the end; who Chooses to work by slow influences; & with whom two thousand years are but as a Single day. Although the Abolitionist must know this, & must See that he has neither the right or power of operating except by moral means & suasion, & if he means well to the slave, he must not Create angry feelings in the Master; that although he may not approve the mode which it pleases Providence to accomplish its purposes, the result will nevertheless be the same; that the reasons he gives for interference in what he has no Concern, holds good for every kind of interference with our neighbors when we disapprove their Conduct; Still I fear he will persevere in his evil Course. Is it not strange

that the descendants of those pilgrim fathers who Crossed the Atlantic to preserve their own freedom of opinion, have always proved themselves intolerant of the Spiritual liberty of others?"
* Robert E. Lee expressing his views on slavery in a letter to his wife, December 27, 1856. Here Lee explains that he believes that slavery is a moral and political evil, but that it's up to God to decide when it should end.

#65. "Order A.P. Hill to prepare for action! Pass the infantry to the front rapidly! Tell Major Hawks--Let us cross over the river and rest under the shade of the trees."
* General Thomas Jonathan "Stonewall" Jackson was struck by friendly fire at the Battle of Chancellorsville the evening of May 2, 1862. His wounds were severe and his left arm was amputated. Jackson was recovering, but then he developed pneumonia. Stonewall was in a delirium as he spoke these last words on May 10, 1862. He was thirty-nine-years-old when he died.

#66. "If we only save the finger of one man, that's enough."
* General James Longstreet at the Battle of Fredericksburg, fought December 11-15, 1862. Union casualties at the Battle of Fredericksburg were 13,353, while Confederate casualties were 4,576. Apparently, Longstreet was referring to saving Confederate fingers, not Union fingers.

#67. "General, I have been a soldier all my life. I have been with soldiers, engaged in fights by squads, companies, regiments, divisions, and armies, and should know, as well as anyone what soldiers can do. It is my opinion that no fifteen thousand men ever arrayed for battle can take that position."
* Confederate General James Longstreet to General Robert E. Lee, voicing his concerns to Lee about an impending attack (known as "Pickett's Charge") on the Union center on Cemetery Ridge, July 3, 1863. Longstreet was known as Lee's "Old War Horse."

#68. "Longstreet opposed Pickett's Charge, and the failure shows he was right. All these damnable lies about Longstreet make me want to shoulder a musket and fight another war. They originated in politics by men not fit to untie his shoestrings. We soldiers on the firing line knew there was no

greater fighter in the whole Confederate army than Longstreet. I am proud that I fought under him here. I know that Longstreet did not fail Lee at Gettysburg or anywhere else. I'll defend him as long as I live."
* Captain O. Hooper, in an interview 75 years after the Battle of Gettysburg regarding Confederate General James Longstreet's opposition to Pickett's Charge on July 3, 1863. Hooper was a survivor of Pickett's Charge.

#69. "Never stand and take a charge. Charge them too."
* General Nathan Bedford Forrest. Forrest began his Civil War military career as a private in the Confederate Army. By the end of the Civil War, he'd advanced all the way up to lieutenant general in rank. As this quote indicates, Nathan Bedford Forrest was an aggressive fighter.

#70. "After all, I think Forrest was the most remarkable man our Civil War produced on either side."
* Union General William Tecumseh Sherman after the Civil War offering his estimation of Confederate Lieutenant General Nathan Bedford Forrest.

#71. "I went into the army worth a million and a half dollars, and came out a beggar."
* Before the Civil War, Confederate Lieutenant General Nathan Bedford Forrest made a fortune as a slave trader, a planter, and by investing in real estate. Forrest spent his own money to help his men acquire supplies.

#72. "The massacre at Fort Pillow occurred April 12, 1864, and has been the subject of congressional inquiry. No doubt Forrest's men acted like a set of barbarians, shooting down the helpless negro garrison after the fort was in their possession; but I am told that Forrest personally disclaims any active participation in the assault, and that he stopped the firing as soon as he could. I also take it for granted that Forrest did not lead the assault in person, and consequently that he was to the rear, out of sight if not of hearing at the time, and I was told by hundreds of our men, who were at various times prisoners in Forrest's possession, that he was usually very kind to them. He had a desperate set of fellows under him, and at that very time there is no doubt the feeling of the Southern people was fearfully savage on this very point of our making soldiers out of their late slaves, and

501 Civil War Quotes and Notes

Forrest may have shared the feeling."
* William Tecumseh Sherman, from his book *Memoirs of General W.T. Sherman*. At Fort Pillow there was a massacre of black Union soldiers, Tennessee Unionists, and Confederate deserters, all who had surrendered. Controversy continues today about Nathan Bedford Forrest's role in what happened at Fort Pillow.

#73. "The slaughter was awful. Words cannot describe the scene. The poor, deluded, negroes would run up to our men, fall upon their knees, and with uplifted hands scream for mercy, but they were ordered to their feet and then shot down. I, with several others, tried to stop the butchery, and at one time had partially succeeded, but General Forrest ordered them shot down like dogs and the carnage continued. Finally our men became sick of blood and the firing ceased."
* Achilles Clark was a Confederate soldier in the 20th Tennessee, he wrote to his sister describing the massacre of African-American Union soldiers at Fort Pillow.

#74. "The poor benighted wretches thought they were heaping indignities upon his dead body; but the act recoils upon them... We can imagine no holier place than where he is."
* Robert Gould Shaw was the white leader of the African-American 54th Massachusetts Infantry at Fort Wagner. This quote is from Robert Gould Shaw's father, when learning that Confederates had tossed his son's body into a mass grave along with the bodies of the African-American soldiers who died at Fort Wagner in July 1863.

#75. "It ain't so hard to get to that ridge -- The hell of it is to stay there."
* A Confederate soldier prior to Pickett's Charge at the Battle of Gettysburg, July 3, 1863.

#76. "You see what a poor sinner I am, and how unworthy to possess what was given me; for that reason it has been taken away."
* An excerpt from a letter Robert E. Lee wrote to his daughter after their family home of Arlington was taken by the Yankees, December 25, 1861. At the time, Lee was on duty on the coast of South Carolina at Coosawhatchie.

Go ahead, say "Coosawhatchie" out loud, you know you want to.

#77. "Its huge doors swung open and we were in the presence of — I do not know what to call them. It was evident they were human beings but hunger, sickness, exposure and dirt had so transformed them that they more resembled walking skeletons, painted black."
* Union Sergeant Lucius Barber, regarding the appearance of the Yankee prisoners of war at Andersonville Prison, Georgia.

#78. "I should be glad if I came as near to the central idea of the occasion in two hours as you did in two minutes."
* Orator Edward Everett in a letter to President Abraham Lincoln referring to Lincoln's Gettysburg Address. Everett was the keynote speaker at the dedication of the National Cemetery in Gettysburg, Pennsylvania on November 19, 1863.

#79. "I failed, I failed, and that is about all that can be said about it."
* President Abraham Lincoln's self-criticism of his famous Gettysburg Address. We know the Gettysburg Address was not a failure. It is one of the greatest speeches ever made.

#80. "It's bad. It's damned bad."
* President Abraham Lincoln's reaction to the Union Army's defeat at First Bull Run (First Manassas) after a congressman asked him how the battle went.

#81. "I beg to present you as a Christmas gift the city of Savannah."
* General William Tecumseh Sherman, from a wire to President Abraham Lincoln on December 22, 1864. Sherman captured Savannah, Georgia after his March to the Sea from Atlanta. Savannah was an important port and its loss weakened the Confederacy.

#82. "They couldn't hit an elephant at this distance."
* It is accepted that General John Sedgwick spoke these last words just

moments before being shot dead by a Confederate sniper at Spotsylvania. There is more to this quote that should be considered for accuracy's sake. Sedgwick was reviewing his lines at Spotsylvania while he and his men were under fire from snipers, he became annoyed with his men trying to avoid the sniper fire by constantly jumping and diving about, a mostly useless effort. This is when he said; "They couldn't hit an elephant at this distance." It was then minutes later that he was struck and killed by sniper's bullet. You will sometimes see this quote humorously shortened to; "They couldn't hit an elephant at this dist—"

#83. "He looked as though he ought to have been, and was, the monarch of the world."
* A description of General Robert E. Lee.

#84. "Will you pardon me for asking what the horses of your army have done since the battle of Antietam that fatigues anything?"
* President Abraham Lincoln to General George B. McClellan. McClellan had excused his lack of action in the fall of 1862 because of exhausted horses. He was soon removed from command.

#85. "By some strange operation of magic I seem to have become the power of the land."
* General George McClellan said this of himself shortly after he assumed command of the Union forces around Washington in 1861.

#86. "He will take more chances, and take them quicker, than any other general in the country — North or South."
* A contemporary speaking of Confederate General Robert E. Lee.

#87. "War is cruelty. There is no use trying to reform it. The crueler it is, the sooner it will be over."
* Union General William Tecumseh Sherman said this to a Southern lady who had criticized Sherman for actions of his troops during the Meridian Campaign. This was shortly before Sherman began his brutal March to the Sea. Compare this quote to the first sentence of the second paragraph of

quote #52.

#88. "It's just like shooting squirrels, only these squirrels have guns—that's all."
* The advice from a Union private, who had experience fighting at Fort Donelson, to new recruits from Ohio. The Ohioans were under fire for the first time and their colonel had skedaddled off to the rear when the firing began. This experienced private from another regiment came to instruct the green Ohio men on how to load their muskets. With the private's help, the Ohioans kept up their fire and held their position.

#89. "Boys, he's not much for looks, but if we'd had him we wouldn't be caught in this trap."
* A captured Union soldier describing Confederate General Thomas Jonathan "Stonewall" Jackson.

#90. "Find out where your enemy is. Get at him as soon as you can, and strike him as hard as you can. And keep moving on!"
* General Ulysses S. Grant, before his Tennessee River Campaign in early 1862. This is Grant's war philosophy in a nutshell.

#91. "I must express my distaste at being commanded by a man with no pretension of gentility. Forrest may be... the best cavalry officer in the West, but I object to a tyrannical, hot-headed vulgarian commanding me."
* A Mississippian describing Nathan Bedford Forrest.

#92.
"That old man... had my division massacred at Gettysburg!"
* George Pickett said these words to John S. Mosby shortly after paying a visit to Robert E. Lee in Richmond after the Civil War.

"Well, it made you famous."
* Mosby's reply to Pickett.

#93. "The time for compromise has now passed, and the South is determined to maintain her position, and make all who oppose her smell Southern powder and feel Southern steel."
* Jefferson Davis was elected provisional president of the Confederate States of America on February 9, 1861, in Montgomery, Alabama. A week afterward, Davis spoke these words as he addressed a crowd in Montgomery.

#94. "I can make men follow me to hell."
* Union General Philip Kearny evaluating his own leadership ability. Kearny was killed on September 1, 1862, during the Battle of Chantilly.

#95. "Notwithstanding the troubles across the river, there is really no crisis, springing from anything in the government itself. In plain words, there is really no crisis except an artificial one! What is there now to warrant the condition of affairs presented by our friends "over the river?" Take even their own view of the questions involved, and there is nothing to justify the course which they are pursuing. I repeat it, then---there is no crisis, excepting such a one as may be gotten up at any time by designing politicians. My advice, then, under such circumstances, is to keep cool. If the great American people will only keep their temper, on both sides of the line, the troubles will come to an end, and the question which now distracts the country will be settled just as surely as all other difficulties of like character which have originated in this government have been adjusted. Let the people on both sides keep their self-possession, and just as other clouds have cleared away in due time, so will this, and this great nation shall continue to prosper as heretofore. But, fellow citizens, I have spoken longer on this subject than I had intended in the outset---and I shall say no more at present."
* Abraham Lincoln's words from a speech given in Pittsburgh, Pennsylvania, on February 15, 1861. Lincoln was en-route to his inauguration.

Below is another Lincoln quote made on the same day, which is very similar to the above quote:

"Frequent allusion is made to the excitement at present existing in our national politics, and it is as well that I should also allude to it here. I think

that there is no occasion for any excitement. The crisis, as it is called, is altogether an artificial crisis.... As I said before, this crisis is all artificial! It has no foundation in fact. It was not 'argued up,' as the saying is, and cannot be argued down. Let it alone, and it will go down itself."
* Abraham Lincoln's words from a speech given in Cleveland, Ohio on February 15, 1861, while Lincoln was en-route to his inauguration.

#96. "A damned old goggle-eyed snapping turtle."
* A soldier's description of Union General George Meade. Meade had a reputation for having a bad temper.

#97. "Tonight we will water our horses in the Tennessee River."
* Confederate General Albert Sidney Johnston said this on April 6, 1862, at the Battle of Shiloh. The Confederates lost at Shiloh, Johnston was killed, and the rebel horses did not get to drink Tennessee River water.

#98. "I know the hole he went in at, but I can't tell you what hole he will come out of."
* President Abraham Lincoln speaking to General William Tecumseh Sherman's brother John, about the destination of Sherman's March to the Sea. John Sherman was a senator from Ohio.

#99. "Do you see those colors? Take them!"
* Union General Winfield S. Hancock gave this order to Colonel William Colville of the 1st Minnesota on July 2, 1863, at the Battle of Gettysburg. The soldiers from Minnesota carried out the order and took the enemy colors, but at a high cost. One-third of the 1st Minnesota's men were lost.

#100. "With this honor devolves upon you also a corresponding responsibility. As the country herein trusts you, so under God it will sustain you."
* President Abraham Lincoln, words used during a ceremony on March 9, 1864, to confer upon Ulysses S. Grant the army's highest rank of lieutenant general.

Here is Grant's response:

"With the aid of the noble armies that have fought on so many fields for our common country, it will be my earnest endeavor not to disappoint your expectations. I feel the full weight of the responsibilities now devolving on me and know that if they are met it will be due to those armies and above all to the favor of that Providence which leads both Nations and men."

#101. "If you don't have my army supplied, and keep it supplied, we'll eat your mules up, sir."
* General William Tecumseh Sherman's warning to an army quartermaster before the departure of Sherman's army from Chattanooga toward Atlanta.

#102. "I can only say that I am nothing but a poor sinner, trusting in Christ alone for salvation."
* General Robert E. Lee, to his army's chaplains.

#103. "Really, Mr. Lincoln, I have had enough of this show business."
* General Ulysses S. Grant, declining an invitation to attend a White House party in his honor, so that he may instead return to the front.

#104. "The rebels are out there thicker than fleas on a dog's back!!"
* An excited Union officer reporting the advance of Confederate forces at Shiloh.

#105. "The Rebel army is now the legitimate property of the Army of the Potomac."
* General Joseph "Fighting Joe" Hooker, before he was soundly defeated by Robert E. Lee at Chancellorsville.

Thomas Jonathan "Stonewall" Jackson

#106. "Pray excuse me. I cannot take it."
* Former Confederate President Jefferson Davis' last words. Spoken in response to his wife Varina's attempt to give him medicine shortly before he died on December 6, 1889, at age 81.

#107. "Hello, Massa; bottom rail on top dis time."
* An African-American Union soldier to his former master, who was now a prisoner of the Yankees.

#108. "June 3. Cold Harbor. I am killed."
* These words were written in a notebook found on the battlefield at Cold Harbor. The notebook belonged to a Union Soldier.

#109. "Strike the tent!"
* The last words of a delirious Robert E. Lee shortly before he died on October 12, 1870. "Strike the tent" means to take the tent down. There is debate about whether or not these were actually Robert E. Lee's last words. Robert E. Lee's biographer, Douglas Southall Freeman, included these as Lee's last words in his well-regarded book; *R. E. Lee: A Biography*. However, Emory Thomas is another noted Lee biographer and he writes in his *Robert E. Lee: A Biography,* that Lee's last words sometime on his last day were: "I will give that sum." Thomas says that no one present at Lee's death knew what he meant.

#110. "Send for a clergyman, I wish to be baptized. I have been basely murdered."
* The last words of General William Nelson, the commander of the Union Army of Kentucky. Nelson was fatally shot by a fellow officer, General Jefferson C. Davis, during an argument in Louisville in 1862.

#111. "Our Southern brethren have done grievously, they have rebelled and have attacked their father's house and their loyal brothers. They must be punished and brought back, but this necessity breaks my heart."
* Major Robert Anderson expressing his assessment of the conflict between North and South. Anderson was the defender of Fort Sumter, April 1861.

#112. "It will be all right if it turns out all right. If not someone will suffer."
* General Ulysses S. Grant's comments while watching soldiers of the Army of the Cumberland attack Missionary Ridge near Chattanooga, Tennessee on November 25, 1863. Grant saw the men making a foolhardy charge up the ridge and thought the result would be disastrous. He questioned Generals George Henry Thomas and Gordon Granger about who had given the order for such a move. General Grant was told that no officer had given an order for the charge, the soldiers were making the attack on their own. The impromptu and unordered attack on Missionary Ridge by the soldiers was a success. Afterward, when an officer congratulated Grant, Grant replied, "Damn the battle! I had nothing to do with it."

#113. "You are green, it is true; but they are green also. You are all green alike."
* President Abraham Lincoln to General Irvin McDowell regarding the inexperience of the Union and Confederate Armies early in the Civil War. This was shortly before First Manassas and Lincoln was urging McDowell to attack the Confederates.

#114. "I shall come out of this fight a live major general or a dead brigadier."
* Confederate Brigadier General Albert Perrin before the Battle of Spotsylvania. Unfortunately for Perrin, advancement in rank did not come his way. He became a dead brigadier general in this fight.

#115. "General, get up--dress quick--you are a prisoner!"
* Confederate partisan John Singleton Mosby led his Mosby's Rangers (or Mosby's Raiders) in March 1863 on a raid behind Union lines near the Fairfax County Virginia courthouse. During the bold raid Mosby, who was known as the Gray Ghost, captured Union General Edwin H. Stoughton after rousing him from his bed at Union headquarters. Mosby said in his memoirs that he gave Stoughton a "spank on his bare back" to wake him. Mosby's raid was quite prosperous, he and his rangers captured fifty-eight horses, thirty enlisted men, two captains, and one Union general in the person of Stoughton. All this without a single shot being fired.

#116. "The Father of Waters again goes unvexed to the sea."
* President Abraham Lincoln in July 1863 after hearing that Federal forces had control of the Mississippi River. Fort Henry, Fort Donelson, Island #10, Fort Pillow, Memphis, Shiloh, Corinth, Holly Springs, Chickasaw Bluffs, Arkansas Post, Grand Gulf, Raymond, Jackson, Champion Hill, Vicksburg, and Port Hudson, were all part of a steady progression of victories in the West for the Union since the start of the Civil War. Vicksburg was taken by General Ulysses S. Grant on July 4, 1863, and now "The Father of Waters," as Lincoln refers to the Mississippi River in this quote, is under Union control. General George Gordon Meade and the Army of the Potomac defeated General Robert E. Lee and his Army of Northern Virginia the day before at the Battle of Gettysburg.

#117. "Permit me to say that the unprecedented measure you propose transcends, in studied and ingenious cruelty, all acts ever brought to my attention in the dark history of war. In the name of God and humanity I protest!"
* Confederate General John Bell Hood's complaint following General William T. Sherman's orders to the citizens of Atlanta to leave the city after its capture by Union forces. Sherman had a response for Hood:

"In the name of common sense, I ask you not to appeal to a just God in such a sacrilegious manner. You who, in the midst of peace and prosperity, have plunged a nation into war — dark and cruel war — who dared and badgered us to battle, insulted our flag, seized our arsenals and forts." [Sherman continued with a long list of bad deeds by the Confederates which is not included here for brevity's sake.] "Talk thus to the marines, but not to me, who have seen these things.... If we must be enemies, let us be men and fight it out as we propose to do, and not deal in such hypocritical appeals to God and humanity. God will judge us in due time, and he will pronounce whether it be more humane to fight with a town full of women and the families of a brave people at our backs, or to remove them to places of safety among their own friends."

#118. "Lee's army will be your objective point. Wherever Lee goes, there you will go also."

* General Ulysses S. Grant's order to General George Meade, commander of the Army of the Potomac, upon Grant's arrival in Virginia in 1864.

#119. "General, if you put every [Union soldier] now on the other side of the Potomac on that field to approach me over the same line, I will kill them all before they reach my line. Look to your right; you are in some danger there but not on my line."
* General James Longstreet to General Robert E. Lee as countless Federal assaults were beaten back by Longstreet's men at the Battle of Fredericksburg.

#120. "If you surrender you shall be treated as prisoners of war, but if I have to storm your works you may expect no quarter."
* General Nathan Bedford Forrest. Forrest commonly issued this warning to opposing forces, he often received a surrender.

#121. "In the time I am writing every stalk of corn in the northern and greater part of the field was cut as closely as could have been done with a knife, and the slain lay in rows precisely as they stood in their ranks a few minutes before. It was never my fortune to witness a more bloody, dismal battle-field."
* Major General Joseph Hooker was the commander of the Union I Corps at Antietam. This is his description of the destruction of a Confederate force that was posted in the cornfield on September 17, 1862.

#122. "I do not want to make this charge; I don't believe it can succeed. I would stop Pickett now, but that General Lee has ordered it and expects it."
* General James Longstreet expressing his doubts to Edward Porter Alexander regarding Pickett's Charge as Pickett's troops moved forward to begin the infamous assault on July 3, 1863. Porter's artillery had previously staged a two-hour bombardment of the Union position on Cemetery Ridge.

#123. "Where is my little boy?"
* Robert E. Lee's son, Captain Robert E. Lee, told a story of when his father returned from the Mexican War after a two-year absence from the family.

At the time, the very young and little Robert was wearing a frock or a blouse, and his hair was curled. A friend of Mary Lee's had stopped by to visit and with her was her son of the same approximate age, dress, hair, and appearance as young Robert. The two young boys were playing together away from the adults when Robert E. Lee arrived back home at Arlington after the Mexican War. Lee was being happily greeted by everyone when he noticed the two young boys, he was anxious to see his son again so he made his way through the greeters toward the children and exclaimed, "Where is my little boy?" Lee then bent over and lifts young Robert's play companion up in the air and kisses him. It had been two years and Lee's son had grown and changed, but Robert E. Lee the young son always remembered the shock and humiliation of the mix-up.

#124. "Whoever saw a dead cavalryman?"
* Infantry troops common criticism of cavalry. Cavalry were said to fight so seldom that they hardly ever had casualties.

#125. "If you bring these leaders to trial it will condemn the North, for by the Constitution secession is not rebellion. Lincoln wanted Jefferson Davis to escape, and he was right. His capture was a mistake. His trial will be a greater one. We cannot convict him of treason. Secession is settled."
* Chief Justice of the United States Supreme Court Salmon P. Chase's private opinion regarding charging former Confederate President Jefferson Davis with treason. Davis was captured on May 10, 1865, at Irwinville, Georgia by Union cavalry. He was indicted for treason, but he never went to trial. Davis spent two years in prison at Fort Monroe, Virginia before being released in May 1867.

#126. "The dead covered more than five acres of ground about as thickly as they could be laid."
* An Alabama colonel describing the Union dead at the Battle of Cold Harbor in 1864.

#127. "I have seen your dispatch expressing your unwillingness to break your hold where you are. Neither am I willing. Hold on with a bull-dog grip and chew & choke as much as possible."

* President Abraham Lincoln offered this advice in a wire to General Ulysses S. Grant during the Siege of Petersburg in 1864-1865. Grant remarked to aides that, "The president has more nerve than any of his advisers."

#128. "I hear constantly of taking strong positions and holding them, — of lines of retreat and of bases of supplies. Let us discard such ideas. The strongest position a soldier should desire to occupy is one from which he can most easily advance against the enemy. Let us study the probable lines of retreat of our opponents, and leave our own to take care of themselves. Let us look before us and not behind. Success and glory are in the advance. Disaster and shame lurk in the rear."
* Union General John Pope to his troops before his sound defeat at the Battle of Second Manassas.

#129. "If God now wills the removal of a great wrong, and wills also that we of the North as well as you of the South, shall pay fairly for our complicity in that wrong, impartial history will find therein new cause to attest and revere the justice and goodness of God."
* Excerpt from an April 4, 1864, letter President Abraham Lincoln sent to Kentuckian Albert Hodge. Hodge was editor of the *Frankfort Commonwealth* newspaper.

#130. "Captain, my religious belief teaches me to feel as safe in battle as in bed. God has fixed the time for my death. I do not concern myself about that, but to always be ready, no matter when it may overtake me."
* General Thomas Jonathan "Stonewall" Jackson's reply to an officer who inquired as to how he remained so calm in battle. Stonewall would die on May 10, 1863, after being mistakenly shot by his own men on May 2 at the Battle of Chancellorsville.

#131. "General, unless he offers us honorable terms, come back and let us fight it out!"
* General James Longstreet to General Robert E. Lee as Lee rode off to discuss terms for surrender with General Ulysses S. Grant. On April 9, 1865, in the parlor of Wilmer McLean's house at Appomattox Court House,

Virginia, Robert E. Lee surrendered the Army of Northern Virginia to Ulysses S. Grant.

#132. "I am now considered such a monster, that I hesitate to darken with my shadow, the doors of those I love, lest I should bring upon them misfortune."
* Ten months after his surrender at Appomattox Court House former Confederate General Robert E. Lee was in Washington D.C., and after the carnage and destruction of the Civil War, Lee was not a popular man in this city. The former Army of Northern Virginia commander was despised and hated in Washington. Lee made this remark to explain why he chose not to visit with his friends who lived in Washington. He knew any visits by him to his Washington friends would only cause them hardship and trouble.

#133. "We are not only fighting hostile armies but a hostile people, and must make old and young, rich and poor, feel the hard hand of war, as well as their organized armies, I know that this recent movement of mine through Georgia has had a wonderful effect in this respect.... The truth is, the whole army is burning with an insatiable desire to wreak vengeance upon South Carolina. I almost tremble for her, but feel that she deserves all that seems in store."
* General William T. Sherman writing to Chief of Staff Henry Halleck on December 24, 1864. Sherman had completed his March to the Sea, now he was preparing to march his army into South Carolina.

#134. "Stand by General Burnside as you have stood by me and all will be well."
* General George Brinton McClellan's advice to his troops in November 1862 after he was replaced in command by Major General Ambrose Burnside.

#135. "I am short a cheek-bone and an ear, but am able to whip all hell yet."
* Union General John M. Corse in a wig-wag message to General William Tecumseh Sherman, after Corse had sustained a wound at the Battle of Allatoona in 1864. It turned out that Corse's wound was not as serious as he let on, he was only grazed by a bullet. Wig-wag was a way to communicate

by waving arms, flags, or other items about in order to send messages back and forth between those who are too distant to be heard but can be seen. Wig-wag was similar to semaphore.

#136. "It is a good face. It is the face of a noble, brave man. I am glad this war is over at last."
* A comment by President Abraham Lincoln as he had breakfast on April 14, 1865, when his son Robert gave him a cartes de visite (a photograph portrait mounted on a card) of General Robert E. Lee. Robert Lincoln served on General Ulysses Grant's staff and was present at Appomattox Court House when Lee surrendered to Grant. Lee gave Robert the cartes de visite of himself as a souvenir. It was Good Friday and that evening President Abraham Lincoln would attend a play where an assassin waited.

#137. "...I believe it to be the duty of everyone to unite in the restoration of the country, and the re-establishment of peace and harmony.... It appears to me that the allayment of passion, the dissipation of prejudice, and the restoration of reason, will alone enable the people of the country to acquire a true knowledge and form a correct judgment of the events the last four years. It will, I think, be admitted that Mr. Davis has done nothing more than all the citizens of the Southern States, and should not be held accountable for acts performed by them in the exercise of what had been considered by them unquestionable right."
* Robert E. Lee, September 1865.

#138. "We talked the matter over and could have settled the war in thirty minutes had it been left to us."
* A Johnny Reb's comment after meeting with a Billy Yank during an informal truce while they sat together on a log. The Confederates were often short of coffee and the Yankees were often short of tobacco. The enemies would sometime fraternize between the lines to trade coffee and tobacco.

#139. "Very commendable, very commendable."
* General Thomas Jonathan "Stonewall" Jackson. Stonewall was looking for his young courier during a battle, but could not find him. Jackson was then told the courier had been killed while performing his duty. General

Jackson replied with this remark.

#140.
"In glades they meet skull after skull
Where pine-cones lay--the rusted gun,
Green shoes full of bones, the mouldering coat
And cuddled-up skeleton;
And scores of such. Some start as in dreams,
And comrades lost bemoan:
By the edge of those wilds Stonewall had charged--
But the Year and the Man were gone."
* An excerpt from Herman Melville's poem, "The Armies of the
Wilderness."

#141. "I am now 105 miles from Chattanooga, and all our provisions have
come over that single road, which is almost daily broken somewhere, but
thus far our supplies have been ample. We have devoured the land and our
animals eat up the wheat and corn field close. All the people retire before us
and desolation is behind. To realize what war is one should follow our
tracks.

"Though not conscious of danger at this moment, I know the country
swarms with thousands who would shoot me, and thank their God they had
slain a monster; and yet I have been more kindly disposed to the people of
the South than any general officer of the whole army."
* General William Tecumseh Sherman writing from the field while near
Marietta, Georgia on June 26, 1864.

#142. "After the fighting was over, where oh where was all the fine rigging
heretofore on our officers? They could not be seen. Corporals, Sergeants,
Lieutenants, Captains, all had torn all the fine lace of their clothing. I
noticed that at the time and was surprised and hurt. I asked several of them
why they had torn the insignia of their rank, and they always answered,
"Humph, you think that I was going to be a target for Yankees to shoot at?"
You see this was our first battle, and the officers had not found out that
minnie as well as cannon balls were blind; that they had no eyes and could
not see. They thought that the balls would hunt for them and not hurt the

privates. I always shoot at privates. It was they that did the shooting and killing, and if I could kill or wound a private, why, my chances were so much the better. I always looked upon officers as harmless personages. Colonel Field, I suppose, was about the only Colonel of the war that did as much shooting as the private soldier. If I shot at an officer, it was at long range, but when we got down to close quarters I always tried to kill those that were trying to kill me."
* Confederate Private Sam Watkins explaining his philosophy for choosing which particular targets to shoot at during the Civil War. Sam Watkins was a member of Company H of the 1st Tennessee Infantry Regiment, Army of Northern Virginia and he fought in many battles during the Civil War. In 1881, Watkins wrote about his experiences in the Civil War and these writings were published as a serial column in *The Columbia Herald* (Tennessee) newspaper. They were later published as a book named *Co. Aytch* which is how Watkins spelled Company H. Here, Watkins is writing after the Battle of Cheat Mountain which was fought in Virginia from September 12 to 15, 1861. The battle was a Union victory.

#143. "I think that Lee should have been hanged. It was all the worse that he was a good man and a fine character and acted conscientiously... It's always the good men who do the most harm in the world."
* Henry Adams. After the Civil War Robert E. Lee became president of Washington College in Lexington, Virginia.

#144. "Students have all gone to war. College suspended. And God help the right."
* From the Registrar's journal of Centenary College early in the Civil War. The Civil War took many young men away from their schooling and studies.

#145. "There is a kind of vindictive spirit that impels me to want to engage in the service of my Country right away. I feel that I would like to shoot a yankee, and yet I know that this would not be in harmony with the spirit of Christianity, that teaches us to love our enemies & do good to them that despitefully use us and entreat us."
* William L. Nugent of Mississippi was twenty-nine-years-old in 1861 when the Civil War began. He enlisted after the first year of the war.

#146. "I have got the best suit of clothes that I had in my life."
* Private Peter Wilson after joining up to fight for the Union with the 1st Iowa Volunteers.

#147. "The negro is the key to the situation—the pivot upon which the whole rebellion turns.... Teach the rebels and traitors that the price they are to pay for the attempt to abolish this government must be the abolition of slavery."
* The advice of former slave and abolitionist Frederick Douglass to President Abraham Lincoln.

#148. "You might as well attempt to put out the flames of a burning house with a squirt-gun. I think this is to be a long war — very long — much longer than any politician thinks. You politicians have got things in a hell of a fix and you may get them out the best you can. I am going to St. Louis to take care of my family, and will have no more to do with it."
* William Tecumseh Sherman assessing the war to his brother John Sherman in 1861. John Sherman was an Ohio senator. In general, William Tecumseh Sherman hated politicians, and he didn't care which party.

#149. "The doll Jack is pardoned. By order of the President. A. Lincoln"
* President Abraham Lincoln, 1862. Willie and Tad Lincoln told their father that their doll "Jack" had been found asleep while on guard duty, this was the president's response to the doll's offense. Doll Jack ought to have been thankful for the President's pardon.

#150. "There is a higher law than the Constitution."
* William H. Seward, from a speech in the United States Senate. Seward was speaking in opposition to a compromise on the issue of slavery. March 11, 1850.

Robert E. Lee

#151. "I am glad to see one real American here."
* General Robert E. Lee to Union Lieutenant Colonel Ely S. Parker during Lee's surrender to General Ulysses S. Grant at Appomattox Court House on April 9, 1865. Parker was a Seneca Indian, a lawyer, an engineer, and an adjutant of Grant's staff. Parker wrote the final draft of the terms of surrender, they were in his handwriting. After Lee's above remark to Ely S. Parker, Parker replied to the Confederate General, "We are all Americans."

#152. "We are scattered, demoralized, stunned— ruined."
* Confederate Mary Chesnut writing in her diary on May 15, 1865. The Civil War was over.

#153. "The questions which for years were in dispute between the State and General Government, and which unhappily were not decided by the dictates of reason, but referred to the decision of war, having been decided against us, it is the part of wisdom to acquiesce in the result, and of candor to recognize the fact."
* Robert E. Lee writing on August 28, 1865, in a letter to John Letcher, who was now the former governor of Virginia.

#154. "The only question on which we did not agree has been settled, and the Lord has decided against me."
* Robert E. Lee after the Civil War.

#155. "What a cruel thing is war; to separate and destroy families and friends, and mar the purest joys and happiness God has granted us in this world; to fill our hearts with hatred instead of love for our neighbours, and to devastate the fair face of this beautiful world! I pray that, on this day when only peace and good-will are preached to mankind, better thoughts may fill the hearts of our enemies and turn them to peace. ... My heart bleeds at the death of every one of our gallant men."
* The Battle of Fredericksburg was fought on December 11-15, 1862. Fredericksburg was a Confederate victory and it was a slaughter of Union troops. General Ambrose E. Burnside suffered a brutal defeat with an estimated 13,353 casualties, while the Confederates lost an estimated 4,576 casualties. This quote is from a letter General Robert E. Lee wrote to his wife Mary on the Christmas following Fredericksburg.

#156. "I care nothing about that anti-slavery which wants to make the Territories free, while it is unwilling to extend to me, as a man, in the free States, all the rights of a man."
* H. Ford Douglas, an African-American leader from Illinois. From a speech made to abolitionists in Massachusetts on July 4, 1860.

#157. "You slaveholders have lived so long on your plantations with no one to gainsay you and the negroes only look up and worship you that you expect to govern everybody & have it all your way."
* Frances Edmonston to her father and brothers, as entered in her sister Charlotte's diary. November 16, 1860.

#158. "The army was accustomed to mud in its varied forms, knee-deep, hub-deep; but to have it so despairingly deep as to check the discordant, unmusical braying of the mules, as if they feared their mouths would fill, to have it so deep that their ears, wafted above the waste of mud, were the only symbol of animal life, were depths to which the army had now descended for the first time."
* These words from a veteran of the "Mud March." General Ambrose Burnside staged what became known as the "Mud March" on January 20-23, 1863. It was an attempt by Burnside to cross the Rappahannock River and strike at Confederate General Robert E. Lee and the Army of Northern Virginia. Previously, on December 11-15, 1862, Burnside had suffered a bloody defeat at Fredericksburg. The "Mud March" earned its name after two days of rainstorms turned the dirt roads of Virginia into quagmires. Men, equipment, and animals were unable to move in the deep and gooey mud. Some animals and equipment were actually swallowed-up and lost in the mud. Burnside had to give up his march and he was soon relieved of command.

#159. "Negroes belonging to our citizens are not considered subjects of exchange and were not included in my proposition."
* General Robert E. Lee to General Ulysses S. Grant explaining why he will not make prisoner exchanges that include African-American Union prisoners. Early in the Civil War prisoner exchanges were common, but in 1863 a problem arose when the South said that captured African-American

Yankee soldiers would not be treated and exchanged the same as white prisoners. The Confederate reasoning was that these particular prisoners were probably ex-slaves who belonged to their masters and not to the Union Army, so they will not be exchanged. Grant realized that the Union prisoner of war camps held more prisoners than the Confederate prisoner of war camps, he thought this "prisoner gap" was an advantage for the Union because the South did not have as many soldiers as the North. Grant ended prisoner exchanges until the end of the Civil War was in sight.

#160. "A white man takes his slave to Nebraska now; who will inform the negro that he is free? Who will take him before court to test the question of his freedom? In ignorance of his legal emancipation, he is kept chopping, splitting, and plowing."
* Abraham Lincoln in 1854, regarding the Kansas-Nebraska Act.

#161. "Stand with anybody that stands right. Stand with him while he is right and part with him when he goes wrong. Stand with the abolitionist in restoring the Missouri Compromise; and stand against him when he attempts to repeal the fugitive slave law. In the latter case you stand with the southern disunionist. What of that? you are still right."
* Abraham Lincoln, from a speech made at Peoria, Illinois on October 16, 1854, during the Lincoln-Douglas debates. Lincoln was replying to Senator Stephen A. Douglas as they were debating the Kansas-Nebraska Act.

#162. "As I have not used up so much time as I had supposed, I will dwell a little longer upon one or two of these minor topics upon which the Judge has spoken. He has read from my speech in Springfield, in which I say 'that a house divided against itself cannot stand.' Does the Judge say that it can stand? [Laughter follows from the audience.] I don't know whether he does or not. The Judge does not seem to be attending to me just now, but I would like to know if it is his opinion that a house divided against itself can stand. If he does, then there is a question of veracity, not between him and me, but between the Judge and an authority of a somewhat higher character. [Laughter and applause comes from the audience.]"
* Abraham Lincoln's speech from the first Lincoln-Douglas debate on August 21, 1858, at Ottawa, Illinois. Lincoln was responding to a previous speech by Senator Stephen A. Douglas. Many people attended this debate

which began at 2:00 p.m. on an uncomfortable dry and dusty day. Somewhere around 10,000 to 12,000 people were in attendance, there were no seats or bleachers available for them to sit upon.

Earlier in his speech, an interchange between Lincoln and a member of the audience occurred which demonstrates Lincoln's wit and humor:

Lincoln: "Now, gentlemen, I hate to waste my time on such things, but in regard to that general Abolition tilt that Judge Douglas makes, when he says that I was engaged at that time in selling out and abolitionizing the old Whig party - I hope you will permit me to read a part of a printed speech that I made then at Peoria, which will show altogether a different view of the position I took in that contest of 1854."

A holler comes from an audience member: "PUT ON YOUR SPECS!"

Lincoln responds: "Yes, sir, I am obliged to do so. I am no longer a young man. [Laughter erupts from the audience.]"

#163.
Yes we'll rally round the flag, boys, we'll rally once again,
Shouting the battle cry of freedom,
We will rally from the hillside, we'll gather from the plain,
Shouting the battle cry of freedom!

(Chorus)
The Union forever! Hurrah, boys, hurrah!
Down with the traitors, up with the stars;
While we rally round the flag, boys, we rally once again,
Shouting the battle cry of freedom!
We are springing to the call for three hundred thousand more,
Shouting the battle cry of freedom!
And we'll fill the vacant ranks of our brothers gone before,
Shouting the battle cry of freedom!

(Chorus)
We will welcome to our numbers the loyal, true and brave,
Shouting the battle cry of freedom!
And although he may be poor, he shall never be a slave,

Shouting the battle cry of freedom!

(Chorus)
So we're springing to the call from the East and from the West,
Shouting the battle cry of Freedom;
And we'll hurl the rebel crew from the land we love the best,
Shouting the battle cry of Freedom.

(Chorus)

* The lyrics of the Union version of the song, "The Battle-Cry of Freedom" by George Frederick Root (1820-1895). For you Johnny Rebs, here is the Confederate version lyrics:

Our flag is proudly floating on the land and on the main,
Shout, shout the battle cry of Freedom!
Beneath it oft we've conquered, and we'll conquer oft again!
Shout, shout the battle cry of Freedom!

(Chorus)
Our Dixie forever! She's never at a loss!
Down with the eagle and up with the cross
We'll rally 'round the bonny flag, we'll rally once again,
Shout, shout the battle cry of Freedom!
Our gallant boys have marched to the rolling of the drums.
Shout, shout the battle cry of Freedom!
And the leaders in charge cry out, "Come, boys, come!"
Shout, shout the battle cry of Freedom!

(Chorus)
They have laid down their lives on the bloody battle field.
Shout, shout the battle cry of Freedom!
Their motto is resistance – "To the tyrants never yield!"
Shout, shout the battle cry of Freedom!

(Chorus)
While our boys have responded and to the fields have gone.
Shout, shout the battle cry of Freedom!
Our noble women also have aided them at home.
Shout, shout the battle cry of Freedom!

(Chorus)

#164. "The compact which exists between the North and the South is a 'covenant with death and an agreement with hell' — involving both parties in atrocious; criminality; and should be immediately annulled."
* William Lloyd Garrison was an ardent abolitionist who believed that the United States Constitution was a pro-slavery document. These are his words from a meeting of the Massachusetts Anti-Slavery Society in 1843. The "compact" and "covenant" which Garrison refers to in this quote is the Constitution of the United States.

#165. "This government, with its institutions, belongs to the people who inhabit it. Whenever they shall grow weary of the existing government, they can exercise their constitutional right of amending it, or their revolutionary right to dismember or overthrow it."
* Abraham Lincoln speaking at the First Republican State Convention held in Philadelphia June 17-19, 1856, at the Musical Fund Hall.

#166. "All this talk about the dissolution of the Union is humbug-nothing but folly."
* Abraham Lincoln, 1856. The dissolution talk ended up being more than humbug and folly.

#167. "A house divided against itself cannot stand.

"I believe this government cannot endure, permanently half slave and half free.

"I do not expect the union to be dissolved-I do not expect the house to fall-but I do expect it will cease to be divided.

It will become all one thing or all the other."
* Excerpts from Abraham Lincoln's House Divided Speech made on June 16, 1858, when he accepted the Illinois Republican Party's United States senator nomination. Lincoln would lose this election to incumbent Stephen

A. Douglas.

#168. Lincoln: "Oh, Fell, what's the use of talking of me for the Presidency, whilst we have such men as Seward, Chase, and others, who are so much better known?"

Jesse W. Fell: "What the Republican party wants. to insure success in 1860, is a man of popular origin, of acknowledged ability, committed against slavery aggressions, who has no record to defend, and no radicalism of character."

Lincoln: "Fell, I admit the force of much that you say, and admit that I am ambitious, and would like to be President...but there is no such good luck in store for me as the Presidency."
* A conversation between Abraham Lincoln and Jesse W. Fell after Lincoln's loss to Stephen A. Douglas for election to the United States Senate in 1858. Jesse W. Fell was a friend of Abraham Lincoln's, he was an Illinois land owner and businessman.

#169. "Surely no native-born woman loves her country better than I love America. The blood of one of its Revolutionary patriots flows in my veins, and it is the Union for which he pledged "life, fortune, and sacred honor" that I love, not any divided or special section of it."
* A diary entry dated December 1, 1860, by a New Orleans woman known only as "G."

#170. "If the Union can only be maintained by new concessions to the slave holders; if it can only be stuck together and held together by a new drain on the negro's blood; if the North is to forswear the exercise of all rights incompatible with the safety and perpetuity of slavery,...then will every right minded man and woman in the land say, let the Union perish, and perish forever."
* Abolitionist and freed slave Frederick Douglass, 1861.

#171. "Plainly, the central idea of secession, is the essence of anarchy."
* President Abraham Lincoln, from his Inaugural Address on March 4,

1861.

#172. "I am exceedingly anxious that this Union, the Constitution, and the liberties of the people shall be perpetuated in accordance with the original idea for which that struggle was made, and I shall be most happy indeed if I shall be an humble instrument in the hands of the Almighty, and of this, his almost chosen people, for perpetuating the object of that great struggle."
* Abraham Lincoln, from a speech made on February 21, 1861, to the New Jersey Senate.

#173. "The dogmas of the quiet past, are inadequate to the stormy present. The occasion is piled high with difficulty, and we must rise -- with the occasion. As our case is new, so we must think anew, and act anew. We must disentrall ourselves, and then we shall save our country."
* From President Abraham Lincoln's message to Congress on December 1, 1862.

#174. "Physically speaking, we cannot separate. We cannot remove our respective sections from each other, nor build an impassible wall between them. A husband and wife may be divorced; and go out of the presence, and beyond the reach of each other; but the different parts of our country cannot do this."
* From President Abraham Lincoln's Inaugural Address, March 4, 1861.

#175. "And this issue embraces more than the fate of these United States. It presents to the whole family of man the question whether a constitutional republic, or democracy—a government of the people by the same people—can or can not maintain its territorial integrity against its own domestic foes. It presents the question whether discontented individuals, too few in numbers to control administration according to organic law in any case, can always, upon the pretenses made in this case, or on any other pretenses, or arbitrarily without any pretense, break up their government, and thus practically put an end to free government upon the earth. It forces us to ask, Is there in all republics this inherent, fatal weakness? Must a government of necessity be too strong for the liberties of its own people, or too weak to maintain its own existence?"

* President Abraham Lincoln, from a message to Congress on July 4, 1861.

#176. "Masters have tried to make us believe that the Yankees only wished to sell us to Cuba, to get money to carry on the war."
* A slave's comments in September 1861.

#177. "Today I was pressed into service, to make red flannel cartridge-bags for ten-inch columbiads. I basted while Mrs. S sewed, and I felt ashamed to think that I had not the moral courage to say. 'I don't approve of your war and I won't help you, particularly in the murderous part of it.'"
* By a woman who is known only as "G." G was not for the Confederate cause even though she lived in New Orleans, Louisiana. This is her diary entry made on May 10, 1861.

#178. "I am a Virginian, every drop of blood that flows in my veins is Virginian, but my being Virginian, don't make me a Secessionist-it, on the contrary, makes me a Unionist, for I think Va's good, is in holding to the Union, to the Constitution & to the laws."
* Sallie Pendleton Rensselaer writing from the part of Virginia that would become the Union state of West Virginia during the Civil War.

#179. "Desperate valor could accomplish nothing but its own demonstration. Our veterans were hurled back over the stricken field, or left upon it—I too, proud witness and sharer of their fate. I am not of Virginia blood; she is of mine."
* Union General Joshua Lawrence Chamberlain regarding fighting at Petersburg. Chamberlain was badly wounded during a charge on Rives's Salient at Petersburg and his wounds caused him agony the rest of his life. He was awarded the Medal of Honor for his actions at Little Round Top during the Battle of Gettysburg.

#180.
"Thou, too, sail on, O Ship of State!
Sail on, O Union, strong and great!
Humanity with all its fears,
With all the hopes of future years,
Is hanging breathless on thy fate!
We know what Master laid thy keel,
What Workmen wrought thy ribs of steel,
Who made each mast, and sail, and rope,
What anvils rang, what hammers beat,
In what a forge and what a heat
Were shaped the anchors of thy hope!
Fear not each sudden sound and shock,
'Tis of the wave and not the rock;
'Tis but the flapping of the sail,
And not a rent made by the gale!
In spite of rock and tempest's roar,
In spite of false lights on the shore,
Sail on, nor fear to breast the sea!
Our hearts, our hopes, are all with thee.
Our hearts, our hopes, our prayers, our tears,
Our faith triumphant o'er our fears,
Are all with thee, -are all with thee! "
* The 1850 patriotic poem "O Ship of State" by Henry Wadsworth
Longfellow. The abolitionist poet believed the United States was heading
toward a showdown over slavery.

#181. "You must not make an abolitionist out of me. I fear you do not
comprehend my real motives for engaging in my country's service. I will
assure you of one thing that it is not for the emancipation of the African
race I fight. I want nothing to do with the Negro. I want them as far from
me as is possible to conceive. Already we have more colored population in
the northern states than is agreeable or profitable, then why fight for more.
Slavery is acknowledged to be a local institution hence it is governed by
local law. This being the case we the people of the free states have no right
even if we were so disposed to interfere with that "peculiar institution." ...I
would not sleep one night in the "Tented Field" to free every slave in
America if they were to remain on our soil. You can have a more favorable
opinion of the African than I have, it is your right. No Lizzie, I am simply

fighting for the Union as it was given to us. I want nothing more. I will have nothing less. When President Lincoln declares the slaves emancipated I will declare myself no longer an American citizen."

* A Union soldier named George Avery writes to his girlfriend Lizzie Little, on January 26, 1862. Lizzie was an abolitionist and it is very clear that George was not. George was fighting for the preservation of the Union, he was not fighting to free the slaves. Despite their difference in opinion about abolition, the two married in the summer of 1863 while George was home on furlough.

#182. "This war be worse I reckon... for everybody is killing everybody."
* The thoughts of a 95-year-old slave named Aunt Sally. Aunt Sally had been a slave on a Virginia plantation her entire life. She was asked by a journalist in 1863 which war was worse, the Civil War or the Revolutionary War.

#183. "Belleville, Dec. 6, 1863

Hon. A. Lincoln, President &c.
You know I have never agreed with you in politics, but permit to say one thing: Prosecute this war with the utmost vigor and put down this accursed rebellion against God and man and posterity north and south will bless you forever.

Yours truly
Wm H. Underwood"
* A letter from William H. Underwood to President Abraham Lincoln. Underwood and Lincoln had teamed together as lawyers years earlier to defend a St. Louis banker.

#184. "Caution, Sir! I am eternally tired of hearing that word caution. It is nothing but the word of cowardice!"
* Radical abolitionist John Brown, while discussing matters with a neighbor. The neighbor saw a need to give warning to John Brown, so Brown set his neighbor straight.

#185. "I now leave, not knowing when, or whether ever, I may return, with a task before me greater than that which rested upon Washington. Without the assistance of that Divine Being, who ever attended him, I cannot succeed. With that assistance I cannot fail."
* Abraham Lincoln, speaking on February 11, 1861, at a train station in Springfield, Illinois. The President-elect was departing Springfield for his Washington, D.C. inaugural. This was the day before Lincoln's birthday. On the same day in Mississippi, Jefferson Davis was leaving on his journey to Montgomery, Alabama for his inauguration as president of the Confederate States of America.

#186. "In This Temple As In The Hearts Of The People For Whom He Saved The Union The Memory Of Abraham Lincoln Is Enshrined Forever"
* An inscription on the Lincoln Memorial in Washington, D.C.

#187. "Chester July 8th 1861
"Mr. Linkin
"I have called on you for some help I am a widir woman with sixth children I was doing pirty well but since this war bisness commence it has cost me a good bit of truble I am willing to do with less for the sake of are union to stand I want you to please help me a little as I stand badly in need of som help please rite and lit me know direct your letter to

"Mrs. Sarah H Vandergrift
"Chester

"I shall put it to a good use."
* Sarah H. Vandergrift, a widow living in Chester, Pennsylvania, wrote this letter to President Abraham Lincoln asking for his help in an unspecified way. It is not known if Lincoln replied to her, but Sarah was probably hoping for some money.

#188. "I don't think the people of the slave states will ever consider the subject of slavery in its true light till some other argument is resorted to other than moral persuasion."
* Abolitionist John Brown's words, October 1859. On December 2, 1859, John Brown was hanged for treason after seizing the United States Armory

at Harpers Ferry, which must have been part of Brown's plan to present "some other argument" to the slave states.

#189. "Men who live by robbing their fellow-men of their labor and liberty...have by the single act of slaveholding voluntarily placed themselves beyond the laws of justice and of honor...it can never be wrong for the imbruted and whip-scarred slaves, or their friends, to hunt, to harass, and even strike down the traffickers in human flesh."
* Freed slave and abolitionist Frederick Douglass, 1859.

#190. "When I strike, the bees will begin to swarm, and I want you to help hive them."
* John Brown's words to Frederick Douglass before Brown's raid on Harper's Ferry in October 1859. Brown did strike, but unfortunately for him, the "bees" never swarmed. The United States Marines, commanded by Robert E. Lee, did swarm and ended Brown's siege of Harpers Ferry.

#191. "The meteor of the war."
* A line from the poem "The Portent" by Herman Melville, referring to radical abolitionist John Brown. Brown's seizing of the federal arsenal at Harper's Ferry, his capture, and his subsequent hanging, helped to create and intensify the divisions which led to the Civil War.

#192. "He was a superior man. He did not value bodily life in comparison with ideal things. He did not recognize unjust human laws; but resisted them as he was bid. For once we are lifted out of the trivialness and dust of politics into the region of truth and manhood."
* By Henry David Thoreau, in his essay, "A Plea for Captain John Brown," 1859.

#193. "I hear many condemn these men because they were so few. When were the good and the brave ever in a majority?"
* By Henry David Thoreau, in his 1859 essay, "A Plea for Captain John Brown."

#194. "If it is deemed necessary that I should forfeit my life for the furtherance of the ends of justice, and mingle my blood further with the blood of my children and with the blood of millions in this slave country whose rights are disregarded by wicked, cruel, and unjust enactments-I submit; so let it be done."
* John Brown, speaking at his sentencing on November 2, 1859. John Brown would hang for his Harpers Ferry raid.

#195. "I have been whipped, as the saying is, but I am sure I can recover all the lost capital occasioned by that disaster; by only hanging a few moments by the neck; and I feel quite determined to make the utmost possible out of a defeat."
* John Brown to his wife. On December 2, 1859, John Brown was hanged by his neck for more than only "a few moments."

#196. "This is a beautiful country."
* John Brown on his way to the gallows while riding in a wagon and seated on his coffin. December 2, 1859.

#197. "I, John Brown am now quite certain that the crimes of this guilty land will never be purged away but with blood."
* John Brown was silent on the gallows, but he gave this note to a guard. John Brown's note was prophetic. The purging away by blood of our guilty land's crime of slavery began with the start of the Civil War.

#198. "So perish all such enemies of Virginia! All such enemies of the Union! All such foes of the human race!"
* Colonel Preston of the Virginia militia. Preston spoke these words to a crowd gathered to see John Brown hang. A curiosity is that a member of the Virginia militia was an actor named John Wilkes Booth. Booth would later make history when he assassinated President Abraham Lincoln. Included in the crowd to see Brown hang were cadets from the Virginia Military Institute led by Thomas J. Jackson, later to be known as the great "Stonewall Jackson" of the Army of Northern Virginia.

#199. "Had I so interfered in behalf of the rich, the powerful, the intelligent, the so-called great, or in behalf of their friends...and suffered and sacrificed what I have in this interference...every man in this court would have deemed it worthy of reward rather than punishment."
* John Brown, speaking during his sentencing on November 2, 1859.

#200.
Hanging from the beam,
    Slowly swaying (such the law),
Gaunt the shadow on your green,
    Shenandoah!
The cut is on the crown
    (Lo, John Brown),
And the stabs shall heal no more.

Hidden in the cap
    Is the anguish none can draw;
So your future veils its face,
    Shenandoah!
But the streaming beard is shown
    (Weird John Brown),
The meteor of the war.
* The poem "The Portent" by Moby Dick author Herman Melville.

John Brown

#201. Two versions of lyrics of "John Brown's Song" or "John Brown's Body"

"John Brown's Body" - An Early Version

John Brown's body lies a-mouldering in the grave,
John Brown's body lies a-mouldering in the grave,
John Brown's body lies a-mouldering in the grave,
But his soul goes marching on.

Chorus: *Glory, glory, hallelujah,*
Glory, glory, hallelujah,
Glory, glory, hallelujah,
His soul goes marching on.

He's gone to be a soldier in the Army of the Lord,
He's gone to be a soldier in the Army of the Lord,
He's gone to be a soldier in the Army of the Lord,
His soul goes marching on.

(Chorus)

John Brown's knapsack is strapped upon his back,
John Brown's knapsack is strapped upon his back,
John Brown's knapsack is strapped upon his back,
His soul goes marching on.

(Chorus)

John Brown died that the slaves might be free,
John Brown died that the slaves might be free,
John Brown died that the slaves might be free,
His soul goes marching on.

(Chorus)

The stars above in Heaven now are looking kindly down,
The stars above in Heaven now are looking kindly down,
The stars above in Heaven now are looking kindly down,
His soul goes marching on.

(Chorus)

"John Brown's Body" Version By William W. Patton

Old John Brown's body lies moldering in the grave,
While weep the sons of bondage whom he ventured all to save;
But tho he lost his life while struggling for the slave,
His soul is marching on.

Chorus: *Glory, glory, hallelujah,*
Glory, glory, hallelujah,
Glory, glory, hallelujah,
His soul goes marching on.

John Brown was a hero, undaunted, true and brave,
And Kansas knows his valor when he fought her rights to save;
Now, tho the grass grows green above his grave,
His soul is marching on.

(Chorus)

He captured Harper's Ferry, with his nineteen men so few,
And frightened "Old Virginny" till she trembled thru and thru;
They hung him for a traitor, themselves the traitor crew,
But his soul is marching on.

(Chorus).

John Brown was John the Baptist of the Christ we are to see,
Christ who of the bondmen shall the Liberator be,
And soon thruout the Sunny South the slaves shall all be free,
For his soul is marching on.

(Chorus)

The conflict that he heralded he looks from heaven to view,
On the army of the Union with its flag red, white and blue.
And heaven shall ring with anthems o'er the deed they mean to do,

For his soul is marching on.

(Chorus)

Ye soldiers of Freedom, then strike, while strike ye may,
The death blow of oppression in a better time and way,
For the dawn of old John Brown has brightened into day,
And his soul is marching on.

(Chorus)

* Two versions of lyrics of the Union marching song, "John Brown's Song" or "John Brown's Body." The song is sung to the music of the "Battle Hymn of the Republic" by Julia Ward Howe, 1861. Howe used the music of William Steffe's camp song "Say, Brothers, Will You Meet Us" for her "Battle Hymn of the Republic." There are other versions of this song, it's interesting to compare them. These two versions are offered for your consideration.

#202. "Old John Brown...agreed with us thinking slavery wrong. That cannot excuse violence, bloodshed, and treason. It could avail him nothing that he might think himself right."
* Abraham Lincoln.

#203. "Nobody was ever more justly hanged."
* Author Nathaniel Hawthorne on John Brown.

#204. "John Brown's effort was peculiar. It was not a slave insurrection. It was an attempt by white men to get up a revolt among slaves, in which the slaves refused to participate. In fact, it was so absurd, that the slaves, with all their ignorance, saw plainly that it could not succeed."
* Abraham Lincoln, February 1860.

#205. "And Old Brown Old Osawatomie Brown, May trouble you more than ever, when you've nailed his coffin down!"
* Excerpt from Osborne Perry Anderson's: *A Voice from Harper's Ferry: a*

narrative of events at Harper's Ferry, with incidents prior and subsequent to its capture by Captain Brown and his men. Earlier in his abolitionist career, John Brown was in Osawatomie, Kansas where he and four of his sons murdered five pro-slavery men. Osawatomie was Brown's response to the pro-slave raid made on Lawrence, Kansas in 1856.

#206. "Still, to use a coarse, but an expressive figure, broken eggs can not be mended. I have issued the emancipation proclamation, and I can not retract it."
* From a letter President Abraham Lincoln wrote to General John Alexander McClernand on January 8, 1863. Before the Civil War McClernand was an Illinois Democrat and a member of the United States House of Representatives.

#207. "Doubly justified by the absence of wrong on our part, and by wanton aggression on the part of others, there can be no doubt that the courage and patriotism of the people of the Confederate States will be found equal to any measure of defense which honor and security may require."
* Confederate President Jefferson Davis, from his Inaugural Address made on February 18, 1860.

#208. "...the union now subsisting between South Carolina and other States, under the name "The United States of America," is hereby dissolved."
* Text from South Carolina's Ordinance of Secession. It was issued by delegates of the South Carolina Convention meeting in Charleston on December 20, 1860. South Carolina's Ordinance of Secession passed by a unanimous vote of its 169 members. South Carolina was the first state to secede from the Union.

#209. "Oh, it is all folly, madness, a crime against civilization."
* Union Colonel William Tecumseh Sherman upon hearing of South Carolina's secession from the Union. Sherman had lived in the South for nearly twelve years and had a true fondness for it. He would play a major part in the Confederacy's defeat.

#210. "You can never subjugate us; you never can convert the free sons of the soil into vassals, paying tribute to your power, and you never can degrade them into the level of an inferior and servile race. Never, never."
* Louisiana Senator Judah P. Benjamin on December 31, 1860, as he resigned from the United States Senate. Benjamin became Attorney General of the provisional Confederate government, then he became its Secretary of War. Later, Benjamin was Secretary of State for the Confederate States of America. After the South's surrender, he went to England where he practiced law and became Queen's Counsel in 1872.

#211. "I rise, Mr. President, for the purpose of announcing to the Senate that I have satisfactory evidence that the State of Mississippi, by a solemn ordinance of her people in convention assembled, has declared her separation from the United States. Under these circumstances, of course, my functions here are terminated. It has seemed to me proper, however, that I should appear in the Senate to announce that fact to my associates, and I will say but little more."
* Jefferson Davis made this speech on the floor of the United States Senate on January 21, 1861. Mississippi was the sixth state to secede and Davis would become the President of the Confederate States of America.

#212. "Throughout the entire state men went as emissaries of Secession and told the people they must go out of the Union if they did not wish to be deprived of their slaves and rifles by the "Yankees" who would compel them to perform all menial offices...they would exchange position with their negroes and the latter be made their masters."
* War reporter Junius Browne of the *New York Tribune* writing in 1865 of events in Arkansas.

#213. "Two years, and an abyss of horror and hatred, and the blood of our slaughtered brothers crying aloud from the ground, all prohibit that impious union."
* The *Richmond Enquirer* newspaper in 1863, commenting on the possibilities of a reunion of the states.

#214. "[I would] welcome the intelligence tomorrow... that the slaves had risen in the South, and that the sable arms which had been engaged in beautifying and adorning the South, were engaged in spreading death and devastation."
* Frederick Douglass, regarding if violence would be needed in order for the slaves to become free.

#215. "We have heard that threat until we are fatigued with the sound. We consider it now, let me say, as mere brutum fulcrum [brute influence], noise and nothing else."
* Maine's Senator William Fessenden. These comments were made in 1854 regarding the South's continued threats of secession. Fessenden would later become President Abraham Lincoln's Secretary of the Treasury.

#216. "We will resist...we will sacrifice our lives, burn our houses, and convert our sunny South... into a wilderness waste...We of the South will tear this Constitution to pieces, and look to guns for justice."
* Mississippi Congressman Reuben Davis, in 1860. The Civil War made many of Reuben's above promises and threats come true. Davis himself did "look to guns for justice" as he served as a Confederate brigadier general.

#217. "Peaceable secession is an utter impossibility."
* Daniel Webster, in February 1860. Webster was a courtroom lawyer and a politician with a rich record of office holding. He twice served in the United States House of Representatives, first representing New Hampshire, then Massachusetts. Webster also served as a United States Senator from Massachusetts twice, and he was the United States Secretary of State twice.

#218. "[W]omen who had never before concerned themselves with politics, took the daily papers to their rooms...and wept over them."
* Abolitionist Mary Livermore. Livermore was highly intelligent. She graduated from an all-female seminary and then taught at the seminary for two years. Next, she became a tutor on a plantation in Virginia. While working at the plantation, Mary Livermore became an abolitionist after witnessing how cruel the peculiar institution of slavery was.

#219. "We are without doubt on the verge, on the brink of an abyss into which I do not wish to look."
* Alexander Stephens, after Abraham Lincoln was elected president on November 6, 1860. Stephens became the vice-president of the Confederate States of America.

#220. "If there is sufficient manliness at the South to strike for our rights, honor, and safety, in God's name let it be done before the inaugural of Lincoln."
* Florida governor Milton F. Perry, November 9, 1860. Florida voted to secede from the Union on January 10, 1861, before Abraham Lincoln was inaugurated.

#221. "If the South goes to war for slavery, slavery is doomed in this country. To say so is like opposing one drop to a roaring torrent."
* A diary entry made on December 1, 1860, by the New Orleans woman known only as "G."

#222. "The prospect before us in regard to our Slave Property, if we continue to remain in the Union, is nothing less than utter ruin."
* From J. B. Grimball's diary entry of December 17, 1860. Grimball was a South Carolina landowner.

Note: The following quotes #223 - #227, are the prophetic warning words of William Tecumseh Sherman. At the time, Sherman was superintendent of the Louisiana State Seminary and Military Academy. On December 24, 1860, he was dining with the school's professor of Latin and Greek, a gentleman from Virginia named Boyd. A newspaper was brought to them with the news that South Carolina had seceded from the Union on December 20, 1860. When Sherman finished reading the newspaper article, he tossed the newspaper over so his friend could read it. Then Sherman, a cigar-smoking, tall, thin, red-haired, forty-year-old, who was fidgety and feisty, a West Point graduate, and an Ohioan, stood and began to explain to his Latin and Greek professor friend what was in store for the South.

#223. "You people of the South don't know what you are doing. This country will be drenched in blood, and God only knows how it will end."

#224. "The North can make a steam engine, locomotive or railway car; hardly a yard of cloth or a pair of shoes can you make. You are rushing into war with one of the most powerful, ingeniously mechanical and determined people on earth-right at your doors. You are bound to fail. Only in spirit and determination are you prepared for war. In all else you are totally unprepared, with a bad cause to start with."

#225. "You people speak so lightly of war; you don't know what you're talking about. War is a terrible thing!"

#226. "You mistake, too, the people of the North. They are a peaceable people but an earnest people, and they will fight, too. They are not going to let this country be destroyed without a mighty effort to save it...Besides, where are your men and appliances of war to contend against them?"

#227. "At first you will make headway, but as your limited resources begin to fail, shut out from the markets of Europe as you will be, your cause will begin to wane. If your people will but stop and think, they must see that in the end you will surely fail."

#228. "You have got things in a hell of a fix, and you may get them out as best you can!"
* William Tecumseh Sherman to his Ohio senator brother John, regarding the mess that William T. believed the politicians had created.

#229. "Will you suffer yourself to be spit upon in this way? Are you submissionists to the dictation of South Carolina...are you to be called cowards because you do not follow the crazy lead of that crazy state?"
* A 1861 message to anti-secession readers of the *Herald* newspaper in

Wilmington, North Carolina. North Carolina seceded from the Union on May 20, 1861, it was the second-to-last state to secede from the Union.

#230. "I am one of the dull creatures that cannot see the good of secession."
* Robert E. Lee, 1861.

#231. "This step, secession, once taken, can never be recalled. We and our posterity shall see our lovely South desolated by the demon of war."
* Alexander Stephens on January 18, 1861. Stephens became the vice-president of the Confederate States of America.

#232. "Disunion will be her ruin-for if there is war-it will surely be in the South and the whole land desolated and land in waste and slavery will certainly go if the Union is dissolved."
* Kentuckian Johanna Underwood. Kentucky was a slave state but it had strong anti-slavery belief too. It was a Border State during the Civil War. The Border States were slave states that remained in the Union. Maryland, Delaware, and Missouri were also Border States. West Virginia is/can be considered to be a Border State because it became a Union state after it separated from Virginia during the Civil War.

#233. "It will probably end the war."
* The vice-president of the Confederate States of America Alexander Stephens, regarding the secession of Virginia from the Union on April 17, 1861. We know Stephens was wrong, the Civil War would end only after four years of bloodshed.

#234. "I think the South is committing suicide, but my lot is cast with the South and being unable to manage the ship, I intend to face the breakers manfully, and go down with my companions."
* North Carolinian Jonathan Worth, May 1861. Worth was against secession, but he supported the rebel cause.

#235. "Our cause is righteous and must prevail."
* Resolution of McGowan's Brigade of the South Carolina volunteers, 1865.

#236. "The Southern Confederacy is at present a sad country; but President Davis is a good and wise man, and many of the generals and other officers in the army are pious. Then there are many good praying people in the land; so we may hope that our cause will prosper."
* From a 1863 southern publication called *The Geographical Reader for Dixie Children*.

#237. "Go quickly and help fill up the first colored regiment from the North...The case is before you. This is our golden opportunity. Let us accept it...Let us win for ourselves the gratitude of the country, and the best blessings of our posterity through all time."
* Abolitionist Frederick Douglass, from an 1863 speech urging black men to join the army. When the Emancipation Proclamation went into effect on January 1, 1863, it included a provision that allowed African Americans to enlist in the army and navy of the Union. Eventually, about ten percent of the Union army would be African American, about 180,000 men.

#238. "Child! Have patience! it takes a great while to turn about this great ship of State."
* Sojourner Truth to radical abolitionists. Sojourner Truth was born into slavery as Isabella Baumfree. She gained her freedom and then became a traveling preacher. Truth was known as a powerful speaker.

#239. "Jeff Davis is no seceder."
* This was on a badge worn by Varina Summer Davis (Davis's wife), in 1860.

#240. "I thought Magrath and all those fellows were great apes for resigning and I have done it myself. It is an epidemic and very foolish. It reminds me of the Japanese who when insulted rip open their own bowels."
* John H. Hammond of South Carolina, expressing second thoughts about his resignation from the United States Senate.

#241. "We have just carried an election on principles fairly stated to the people. Now we are told in advance, the government shall be broken up, unless we surrender to those we have beaten, before we take the offices. In this they are either attempting to play upon us, or they are in dead earnest. Either way, if we surrender, it is the end of us, and of the government."
* President-elect Abraham Lincoln writing in a letter to Republican Congressman James T. Hale of Pennsylvania on January 11, 1861, regarding a proposed constitutional amendment by Hale. Hale's proposed amendment would bar Congress from abolishing slavery in the territories south of latitude 36 degrees 31 minutes. Hale thought this would appease the South, but Lincoln did not agree and the proposed constitutional amendment was rejected.

#242. "We want the military resources of the South concentrated at once; and above all, our foreign relations ought to be assured as quickly as possible. No attempt at foreign negotiations ought to be made by single States. The condition of weakness and confusion which will result from four or five States is indescribable. Weld them together while they are hot."
* South Carolinian William Trescott Smith urging the formation of the seceded states into a confederacy which would be recognized by foreign powers. January 14, 1861.

#243. "We are without machinery, without means and threatened by a powerful opposition; but I do not despond, and will not shrink from the task imposed on me."
* Jefferson Davis, February 1861.

#244. "Big-man-me-ism reigns supreme & every one thinks every other a jealous fool, or an aspiring knave."
* James H. Hammond. Hammond was a former United States South Carolina senator. These are comments he made at the Confederate Convention held in February 1861, in order to create the Confederate States of America. Hammond was suspicious that some at the convention were operating only for their own self-interest.

#245. "If they had to draw soldiers rations while they staid in Richmond I think they would hurry through a little faster."
* The words of a Confederate soldier in January 1864, expressing his frustration with the slow-operating Confederate Congress.

#246. "Our Congress are a set of blockheads."
* The comment of a disgusted Confederate soldier named Isaac Alexander. February 21, 1864.

#247.
Goober Peas

Sitting by the roadside on a summer's day
Chatting with my mess-mates, passing time away
Lying in the shadows underneath the trees
Goodness, how delicious, eating goober peas.

Peas, peas, peas, peas
Eating goober peas
Goodness, how delicious,
Eating goober peas.

When a horse-man passes, the soldiers have a rule
To cry out their loudest, "Mister, here's your mule!"
But another custom, enchanting-er than these
Is wearing out your grinders, eating goober peas.

Peas, peas, peas, peas
Eating goober peas
Goodness, how delicious,
Eating goober peas.

Just before the battle, the General hears a row
He says "The Yanks are coming, I hear their rifles now."
He looks down the roadway, and what d'ya think he sees?
The Georgia Militia cracking goober peas.

Peas, peas, peas, peas
Eating goober peas
Goodness, how delicious,
Eating goober peas.

I think my song has lasted just about enough.
The subject is interesting, but the rhymes are mighty rough.
I wish the war was over, so free from rags and fleas
We'd kiss our wives and sweethearts, say good-bye to goober peas.

Peas, peas, peas, peas
Eating goober peas
Goodness, how delicious,
Eating goober peas.
* "Goober Peas" was a popular Civil War Confederate song by A. Pinder. Goober peas are peanuts.

#248. "Between him and us the issue is distinct, simple, and inflexible. It is an issue which can only be tried by war, and decided by victory. If we yield we are beaten; if the Southern people fail him, he is beaten."
* A message to Congress by President Abraham Lincoln in December 1864. Lincoln here is referring to Confederate President Jefferson Davis and the issue of secession.

#249. "It might seem, at first thought, to be of little difference whether the present movement at the South be called 'secession' or 'rebellion.' The movers, however, well understood the difference. At the beginning, they knew they could never raise their treason to any respectable magnitude, by any name which implies violation of the law."
* President Abraham Lincoln on July 4, 1861, in a message to Congress while it was being held in special session.

#250. "We have treated them as misled long enough. Now then let us treat them as the Rebels they are."
* Union soldier Rufus Mead Jr., May 1862.

Jefferson Davis

#251.
Away down South in the land of traitors,
Rattlesnakes and alligators,
Right away, come away, right away, come away.
Where cotton's king and men are chattels,
Union boys will win the battles,
Right away, come away, right away, come away.

Chorus: Then we'll all go down to Dixie,
Away, away,
Each Dixie boy must understand
That he must mind his Uncle Sam,
Away, away,
And we'll all go down to Dixie.
Away, away,
And we'll all go down to Dixie.

I wish I was in Baltimore,
I'd make Secession traitors roar,
Right away, come away, right away, come away.
We'll put the traitors all to rout.
I'll bet my boots we'll whip them out,
Right away, come away, right away, come away.

(Chorus)

Oh, may our Stars and Stripes still wave
Forever o'er the free and brave,
Right away, come away, right away, come away.
And let our motto ever be --
"For Union and for Liberty!"
Right away, come away, right away, come away.

(Chorus)

* The mocking lyrics from the Union version of the Confederate song, "Dixie."

#252. "Such a hue and cry-whose fault? Everybody blamed by somebody

else. Only the dead heroes left stiff and stark on the battlefield escape."
 * Mary Chesnut. Chesnut kept a diary during the Civil War which is noted for its quality. She was the wife of Confederate General James Chesnut, Jr.

#253.
Major General Grant
My dear General

I do not remember that you and I ever met personally. I write this now as a grateful acknowledgment for the almost inestimable service you have done the country. I wish to say a word further. When you first reached the vicinity of Vicksburg, I thought you should do, what you finally did -- march the troops across the neck, run the batteries with the transports, and thus go below; and I never had any faith, except a general hope that you knew better than I, that the Yazoo Pass expedition, and the like, could succeed. When you got below, and took Port-Gibson, Grand Gulf, and vicinity, I thought you should go down the river and join Gen. Banks; and when you turned Northward East of the Big Black, I feared it was a mistake. I now wish to make the personal acknowledgment that you were right, and I was wrong.

Yours very truly
A. Lincoln
 * President Abraham Lincoln wrote this letter to General Ulysses Grant on July 13, 1863. Lincoln is congratulating Grant for his victory at Vicksburg on July 4, 1863. As shown in Lincoln's letter, Lincoln thought Grant was making a mistake as to how the Vicksburg campaign should be conducted. Grant's plan was the one implemented and it was successful. Here Lincoln is acknowledging to Grant that he was right.

#254. "Intelligence, patriotism, Christianity, and a firm reliance on Him, who has never yet forsaken this favored land, are still competent to adjust, in the best way, all our present difficulty."
 * From President Abraham Lincoln's First Inaugural Address. March 4, 1861.

#255. "I see every chance of a long, confused and disorganizing civil war,

and I feel no desire to take a hand therein."
* William T. Sherman wrote these words to his wife Ellen. January 1861.

#256. "You rejoiced at the occasion, and were only troubled that there were not three times as many killed in the affair. You were in evident glee-there was no sorrow for the killed nor for the peace of Virginia disturbed-you were rejoicing that by charging Republicans with this thing you might get an advantage on us."
* Abraham Lincoln, March 6, 1860. Lincoln was referring to the Democrat opinion of John Brown's raid on Harpers Ferry in 1859.

#257. "How we can get along without fighting in the midst of all this lawlessness is impossible for me to see."
* Union Captain Abner Doubleday in a letter to his wife. Doubleday was writing from Fort Sumter, South Carolina on April 2, 1861. At 4:30 A.M. on April 12th, the Civil War began with the Confederate bombardment of Fort Sumter. At 7:30 A.M. Captain Doubleday fired the first Union answering round from the fort.

#258. "The firing on that fort will inaugurate a civil war greater than any the world has yet seen... you will lose us every friend at the North. You will wantonly strike a hornet's nest which extends from mountains to ocean. Legions now quiet will swarm out and sting us to death. It is unnecessary. It puts us in the wrong. It is fatal."
* Robert Toombs' words to Jefferson Davis regarding Fort Sumter. Toombs was the Confederate Secretary of State, but he later resigned this position to become a brigadier general and fight in battles for the Confederacy.

#259. "She thinks that the taking of Ft. Sumter will put an end to hostilities as the North will see that the South is in earnest, & is so very unwilling to fight itself!!! She will open her eyes a little when she arrives here & finds every man of her acquaintance enlisted."
* Union supporter Sarah Butler Wister regarding her Confederate sister. April 1861.

#260. "I could not fire the first gun of the war."
* Roger Pryor on why he declined to fire the first shot on Fort Sumter on April 12, 1861. Pryor was a newspaper publisher and a United States congressman before he resigned to join the Confederate army. Pryor was a strong secessionist and he became a Confederate congressman.

#261. "Oh my poor children in the South! Now they will suffer! God knows how they will suffer...Oh to think that I should have lived to see the day when Brother should rise against Brother."
* An Indiana woman after hearing of the bombardment of Fort Sumter. She had children living in both the North and the South.

#262. "A horse on Sullivan's Island was the only living creature deprived of life during the bombardment."
* The *Charleston Press* reporting on the effects of the Fort Sumter bombardment on April 12, 1861. During surrender ceremonies at the fort an accidental powder explosion killed a Federal soldier named Daniel Hough. Although his death was not caused by battle, Hough was the first soldier to be killed in the Civil War. Another soldier died later as a result of injuries from this accidental explosion.

#263. "Fort Sumter is ours, and nobody is hurt. With mortar, Paixhan, and petard, we tender "Old Abe" our Beau-regard."
* A comment in the *Charleston Mercury* newspaper by Confederate President Jefferson Davis on April 16, 1861. It's curious to note that although Davis refers here to Abraham Lincoln as "Old Abe," Davis himself was older than Lincoln. Jefferson Davis was born on June 3, 1808, while Abraham Lincoln was born on February 12, 1809.

#264. "Quarters in Sumter all burned down. White flag up. Have sent a boat to receive surrender. But half an hour before had sent a boat to stop our firing and offer assistance."
* Correspondence on April 13, 1861, at 2:00 P.M. from P.G.T. Beauregard at Charleston, South Carolina to Confederate President Jefferson Davis in Montgomery, Alabama.

#265. "April 13. Here begins a new chapter of my journal entitled WAR."
* George Templeton Strong was a New York City lawyer who kept a diary during the Civil War. Here he writes of what Fort Sumter meant.

#266. "We propose an appropriation of one million dollars to pay for the scalps of rebels."
* A proposal by Samuel E. Brown of the Ohio House of Representatives on April 14, 1861, after Fort Sumter had fallen to the rebels. Brown's proposal did not succeed.

#267. "I am for a war that will either establish or overthrow a Govt., and will purify the atmosphere of political life. We need such a war & we have it now."
* Senator from Ohio John Sherman on April 15, 1861. John Sherman was the younger brother of General William T. Sherman. Later in his political career, John Sherman was President William McKinley's Secretary of the Treasury.

#268. "All good Carolinians are entitled to take the rank of Colonel if they have property enough. In Alabama, if the boat takes a hundred bales from a man's plantation, he is a Colonel. Before the war it required from three hundred to a thousand bales to make him a general."
* Miriam Cohen of Columbia, South Carolina sarcastically commenting on how officer positions were filled in the Confederate Army. Early in the war, in both the North and South, enlisted men elected their officers. Other officers were appointed by governors. Later in the war, officers more often gained their positions based on merit.

#269. "What a change now greets us! The Government is aroused, the dead North is alive, and its divided people united...The cry now is for war, vigorous war, war to the bitter end, and war till the traitors are effectually and permanently put down."
* Frederick Douglass's thoughts in May 1861 after the Civil War began with the bombardment of Fort Sumter.

#270. "Now when bricks begin to fly about violently by tons' weight at a time, which is the case when they come in contact with 15-inch shells, they make themselves very unpleasant to those who have trusted to them for protection. This was conclusively shown at Fort Sumter."
* Captain Fitzgerald Ross, 1865. In April 1862 the masonry-built Confederate Fort Pulaski in Savannah, Georgia was surrendered after a bombardment by Federal rifled cannon. Forts built of stone or brick were made obsolete by the rifled guns used in the Civil War, as both Fort Sumter and Fort Pulaski proved.

#271.
Richard Malcolm Johnston: "Well, the Convention at Charleston has adjourned. What do you think of matters now?"

Alexander Stephens: "Think of them? Why, that men will be cutting one another's throats in a little while. We shall, in less than twelve months, be in a civil war, and that one of the bloodiest in the history of the world. Men seem to be utterly blinded to the future. Their reason has already left them, and in a little while they will be under the complete control of the worst passions."
* Colonel Richard Malcolm Johnston and Alexander Stephens discussing matters in May 1860. Richard Malcolm Johnston was a lawyer, teacher, and humorist from Georgia who had been associated with Alexander Stephens in a law practice. He also wrote *Life of Alexander H. Stephens*.

#272.
"Why, why, why, and why,
And why to the war, young man?"
"Did a man ever fight for a holier cause,
Than Freedom and Flag and Equal Laws?
Just speak your mind quite freely—Now reely."

"Which, which, which, and which,
And which is the Flag of the free?"
"O Washington's Flag, with the stripes and the stars,
Will you give such a name to the thing with the

bars?
I speak my mind quite freely—Now reely."

"Who, who, who, and who,
And who goes with you to the war?"
"Ten thousand brave lads, and if they should
stay here,
The girls would cry shame, and they'd volunteer!
They speak their mind quite freely—now reely."

"When, when, when, and when,
And when do you mean to come back?"
"When the Rebellion is crushed and the Union re-
stored,
And Freedom is safe—yes, then, please the Lord!
I speak my mind quite freely—Now reely."
* The lyrics from a song named "The Why and the Wherefore" used for Union enlistment in the war.

#273. "Every soldier, nearly, had a servant with him, and a whole lot of spoons and forks, so as to live comfortably and elegantly in camp, and finally to make a splurge in Washington when they should arrive there, which they expected would be very soon indeed."
* Mary A. Ward describing Confederate troops as they left Rome, Georgia. Ward was testifying before Congress after the war was over.

#274. "I cannot study, and I wish to join a Horse Company."
* The aspirations of a University of Mississippi student when the Civil War began.

#275. "I would advise all my friends unless the[y] wish to live like negroes to stay at home, I know if there is another war this chicken wont be thar when they enlist."
* A Confederate private from Mississippi named Joe Shields. Shields made these comments on July 1, 1861, when early in the Civil War there was an air of romance about joining up and fighting. As blood was spilled, it became apparent that war was not all romance. Instead, war was a risky

and deadly proposition.

#276. "Your requisition is illegal, unconstitutional, revolutionary, inhuman, diabolical, and cannot be complied with."
* Missouri Governor Claiborne Jackson regarding President Abraham Lincoln's request for troops. It was realized the Civil War was going to last longer than first thought, and that it would require more men. On May 3, 1861, Lincoln began expanding the army. By early 1862, there were more than 700,000 men in the Union army. The idea of a short war requiring only 75,000 militiamen for 90 days of service, had proved to be wrong.

#277. "I changed my business at one time when I was with my master as a waiter-in the rebel service I was with him Eleven month. I came home with him. I told my son what was going on he with 11 more ran off and joined the Army (the Yankee Army) on St Catherine Island."
* From a slave named Samuel Elliot. After the Emancipation Proclamation was issued on January 1, 1863, President Abraham Lincoln called for four black regiments. By the time the Civil War ended, approximately 300,000 African-Americans making up 166 regiments were in service fighting for the Union.

#278. "At the outbreak of the war it was found very difficult to raise infantry in Texas, as no Texan walks a yard if he can help it. Many mounted regiments were therefore organized, and afterward dismounted."
* Comments of Sir Arthur Fremantle, 1863. Fremantle was a British Colonel visitor and observer of the Civil War.

#279. "God has spared me this time. I pray he will spare me to return to you alive and well. I shan't resist."
* It seems that in June 1864, a Union soldier named George H. Bates had had enough of the Civil War.

#280. "I went into the Union service very willingly...my actions feeling and sympathies have all the time been for the success and maintenance of the Union cause & all the time willing and desirous to fight or do any thing else

in my power, in that behalf."
* An African-American Union soldier named Robert Houston.

#281.
"I was a ploughboy in the field,
A gawky, lazy, dodger,
When came the conscript officer
And took me for a sodger.
He put a musket in my hand,
And showed me how to fire it;
I marched and counter-marched all day;
Lord, how I did admire it!"
* These are a few lyrics from a Southern song named "The Valiant Conscript." It's sung to the music of "Yankee Doodle."

#282. "I say emphatically, Kentucky will furnish no troops for the wicked purpose of subduing her sister Southern States."
* Kentucky Governor Beriah Magoffin's thoughts regarding Abraham Lincoln's 1861 call for additional troops. Kentucky was a Border State during the Civil War, it was a slave state that stayed in the Union. Both the North and the South had troops that came from Kentucky.

#283. "This Conscript Act will do away with all the patriotism we have. Whenever men are forced to fight they take no personal interest in it. ...My private opinion is that our Confederacy is gone, or will go soon. ...A more oppressive law was never enacted in the most civilized country or by the worst of despots. Remember what I say it will eventually be our ruin... I am mad at the action of Congress and Jeff Davis and won't deny it."
* A South Carolinian soldier writes home on April 18, 1862, expressing his anger with the Confederate Conscription Act passed on April 16, 1862, by the Confederate States Congress. This act conscripted all white males between the ages of 18 and 35 into service if they were not legally exempt. In September 1862 the upper age limit was raised to 45. The age limits were 17 and 50 by February of 1864. The North had more than three times the number of white men of military age than the South, the South kept needing more and more men to fight the Civil War.

#284. "He put ...[me] in the gard house one time & he got drunk again from Wilmington to Goldsboro on the train & we put him in the Sh-t House So we are even."
* A private from North Carolina is talking about his captain in 1862. Sometimes officers did not have the respect of those they led.

#285. "One of the most surprising results of the conscription was the amount of disease disclosed among men between "eighteen and forty-five" in districts where quotas could not be raised by volunteering."
* An observation made by humorist David Ross Locke. On April 16, 1862, the Confederate States Congress made the Conscription Act. This unpopular act conscripted all white males between the ages of 18 and 35 into service. Later, the upper age limit was raised to 45. Despite their youth, some men tried to avoid being conscripted into service by claiming health problems.

#286. "I do not think it is right for me to go through the hardships of camp life and the danger of Battle and others living at home enjoying life because they have a few Negroes."
* The Confederate Conscription Act allowed some men to be legally exempt. The reasons that some were exempt, made others who were not exempt unhappy. There was an exemption for planters who owned 20 or more slaves. This comment is from an unhappy conscripted Confederate soldier named James Skelton who apparently was not exempt by ownership of slaves.

#287. "I still cannot help feeling it as a strain, a cause for blushing, that he should have a substitute."
* The Confederacy's Conscription Act allowed you to pay $300 or purchase a substitute to avoid the draft. In this quote, Willie Wadley's sister Sarah is commenting on the strain inflicted on her by Willie's ability to secure himself a substitute to fight for him in the war. The Civil War was a source of hardship and sacrifice for all, even for the poor, strained, and blushing Sarah Wadley whose brother obtained a substitute. Perhaps Willie Wadley would have preferred a substitute sister.

#288. "You who do not wish to be soldiers, do not like this law. This is natural; nor does it imply want of patriotism. Nothing can be so just, and necessary, as to make us like it, if it is disagreeable to us."
* President Abraham Lincoln regarding the draft. September 1863.

#289.
"We'll pray for the Conscript with frown on his brow,
To fight for his country, he won't take the vow;
May bad luck and bad fortune him always attend":
'And die with dishonour'-said the Soldier's Amen."
* A song from the Civil War called "The Soldier's Amen."

#290. "To ride up to a man's door, whose hospitable kindness makes you feel welcome & tell him, in the presence of his faithful & loving wife & sunny-faced children, that he must be ready in 10 minutes to go with you...this is indeed a sad and unpleasant task."
* Leonidas L. Polk, 1863. Polk was from North Carolina and he fought for the Confederacy. Polk was also an Episcopal bishop. He was related to President James Polk, and he was friends at West Point with his classmate Jefferson Davis. Polk was killed at Pine Mountain, Georgia on June 14, 1864.

#291. "He liked the war, but didn't like to do his share."
* A Confederate soldier named Edmund Patterson regarding a deserter, March 1863.

#292. "It take one half of the men to keep the other half from running away."
* The thoughts of a Confederate soldier named James Bracy in 1863.

#293. "Must I shoot a simple-minded soldier boy who deserts, while I must not touch a hair of a wiley agitator, who induces him to desert?...I think that in such a case, to silence the agitator, and save the boy, is not only constitutional, but a great mercy."

* President Abraham Lincoln.

#294. "There are few crimes in the sight of either God or man, that are more wicked and detestable than desertion."
* From a sermon given by Chaplain John Paris after the hangings of twenty-two North Carolinian Confederate deserters in February 1864. The Tar Heels were hanged because they were recognized as men who had deserted from Confederate ranks to the Yankees. They were wearing Union uniforms and carrying Yankee muskets when taken prisoner during fighting near New Bern, North Carolina.

#295. "The Deserters were marched around where their graves were dug. Their coffins which was merely rough board boxes were plased over their graves and each one was seated on their own coffins. There each one could see his final resting place."
* A description of an execution of deserters during the Civil War.

#296. "The men seem to think desertion is no crime and hence never shoot a deserter when he goes over-they always shoot but never hit."
* Confederate Luther Rice Mills regarding practices of the troops during the Petersburg siege in 1864.

#297. "General, there are already too many weeping widows in the United States. For God's sake, don't ask me to add to the number, for I won't do it."
* President Abraham Lincoln refusing the request of a Union officer for Lincoln to sign the warrants of execution of 24 deserters.

#298. "We are fighting for independence, and that, or extermination, we will have."
* Confederate States of America President Jefferson Davis.

#299. "He was a warm friend and a bitter enemy...He was a regular bull-dog when he formed an opinion, for he would never let go."
* The comments of a clerk who worked for Confederate President Jefferson

Davis.

#300. "Davis is venal and corrupt, and the Confederate Congress is no better."
* South Carolina Congressman Thomas J. Withers' opinion of Jefferson Davis and the Confederate Congress.

#301. "Mr. Davis is a man of slight, sinewy figure, rather over the middle of height, and of erect, soldier-like bearing. His is about fifty-five years of age; his features are regular and well defined, but the face is thin and marked on cheek and brow with many wrinkles, and is rather careworn and haggard. One eye is apparently blind, the other is dark, piercing, and intelligent. He was dressed very plainly in a light gray summer suit."
* A description of Confederate President Jefferson Davis by a London Times correspondent, May 1861.

#302. "We have made a great mistake in the choice of a president."
* Alabama Congressman Robert Smith, December 1861.

#303.
"Jeff Davis rode a dapple gray,
Lincoln rode a mule,
Jeff Davis is a gentleman,
And Lincoln is a fool."
* A verse from a Confederate song making fun of President Abraham Lincoln.

Ulysses S. Grant

#304. "It is not only honorable to our women to weave and wear their dresses, but really homespun is becoming to them."
* Confederate President Jefferson Davis writing his advice in 1862 to the women in the Milledgeville, Georgia Confederate Union. Southern ladies of upper class and standing did not want to wear homespun. Davis hoped that having the women make their own clothes would help spur the lagging Confederate economy. Plus, the rebel ladies learn here how becoming they are to Jefferson Davis when they wear homespun clothes.

#305. "Jefferson Davis is not only a dishonest man, but a liar."
* The opinion of South Carolina Congressman Robert Barnwell Rhett regarding President Jefferson Davis, April 15, 1864. Rhett was a strong supporter of secession.

#306.
Jeff Davis was a hero bold, You've heard of him, I know
He tried to make himself a king where southern breezes blow.
But "Uncle Sam" he laid the youth across his mighty knee
And spanked him well and that's the end of brave old Jeffy D.

Chorus: *Oh! Jeffy D.!*
You "flow'r of chivalree,"
Oh royal Jeffy D.!
Your empire's but a tin-clad skirt
Oh charming Jeffy D.

This Davis he was always full of bluster and of brag,
He swore, on all our Northern walls he'd plant his Rebel flag.
But when to battle he did go he said, "I'm not so green,
To dodge the bullets I will wear my tin-clad crinoline."

(Chorus)

Now when he saw the game was up he started for the woods,
His bandbox hung upon his arm quite full of fancy goods.
Said Jeff, "They'll never take me now, I'm sure I'll not be seen
They'd never think to look for me beneath my crinoline."

(Chorus)

Jeff took with him, the people say, a mine of golden coin
Which he, from banks and other places managed to purloin.
But while he ran, like every thief, he had to drop the spoons,
And maybe that's the reason why he dropped his pantaloons.

(Chorus)

Our union boys were on his track for many nights and days,
His palpitating heart it beat Enough to burst his stays.
Oh! What a dash he must have cut with form so tall and lean
Just fancy now the "What is it? Dressed up in crinoline!"

(Chorus)

The ditch that Jeff was hunting for he found was very near,
He tried to "shift" his base again, his neck felt rather queer.
Just on the out-"skirts" of a wood his dainty shape was seen,
His boots stuck out, and now they'll hang Old Jeff in crinoline.

(Chorus)
* This song is called "Jeff In Petticoats" and it makes fun of President Jefferson Davis. After the collapse of the Confederacy, Jefferson Davis skedaddled, fleeing for safety and hoping to avoid being caught. There was a rumor that Davis was in disguise and wearing a dress when he was captured by Union cavalry on May 10, 1865.

#307. "Bragg is beyond doubt the best disciplinarian in the South. When he took command at Corinth, the army was little better than a mob."
* From rebel John Buie, September 1862. Buie is referring to General Braxton Bragg. Bragg suffered from migraines or "sick" headaches and was often ill. He was a native North Carolinian and Fort Bragg in North Carolina is named in his honor.

#308. "None of the General Bragg's soldiers ever loved him. They had no faith in his ability as a general. He was looked upon as a merciless tyrant. The soldiers were very scantily fed. Bragg never was a good feeder or

commissary-general. Rations with us were always scar[c]e. No extra rations were ever allowed to the negroes who were with us as servants. No coffee or whiskey or tobacco were ever allowed to be issued to the troops. If they obtained these luxories, they were not from the government. These luxories were withheld in order to crush the very heart ans spirit of his troops. We were crushed. Bragg was the great autocrat. In the mind of the soldier, his word was law. He loved to crush the spirit of his men. The more of a hang-dog look they had about them the better was General Bragg pleased. Not a single soldier in the whole army ever loved or respected him."
* These comments about Confederate General Braxton Bragg by soldier Sam Watkins writing in his book, "Co. Aytch." Braxton Bragg's brother Thomas, was Attorney General for the Confederacy from November 21, 1861, to March 18, of 1862.

#309. "Forrest may be & no doubt is, the best Cav officer in the West, but I object to a tyrannical, hot-headed vulgarian's commanding me."
* From a Confederate soldier named Harry St. John Dixon in 1864. Nathan Bedford Forrest enlisted in the Confederate army as a private shortly before his fortieth birthday. In civilian life, he had built himself up from poverty to become a millionaire. He became a general and used his own money to help fund war efforts of the Confederacy.

#310. "I seem to have a more perfect command of my faculties in the midst of fighting."
* General Thomas Jonathan "Stonewall" Jackson.

#311. "He was the true type of all great soldiers. Like the successful warriors of the world, he did not value human life where he had an object to accomplish. He could order men to their death as a matter of course. His soldiers obeyed him to the death. Faith they had in him stronger than death. Their respect he commanded."
* Mary Chesnut on General Thomas Jonathan "Stonewall" Jackson. On May 2, 1863, at Chancellorsville, Stonewall Jackson was mistakenly shot by his own men and severely wounded. Stonewall's left arm was amputated as a result of the wounds. He lasted eight days but finally died of pneumonia.

#312. "All admire his genius and great deeds; no one could love the man for

himself. He seems to be cut off from his fellow-man and to commune with his own spirits only, or with spirits of which we wot not."
* A Confederate officer writing in August 1862 regarding General Thomas Jonathan "Stonewall" Jackson. Jackson had other nicknames. He picked up "Stonewall" during First Bull Run. At West Point, he was called "Old Jack" and at the Virginia Military Institute, where he was a professor, he was called "Tom Fool Jackson" by the cadets. Soldiers referred to him as "Old Blue Light," "Old Jack," and "Stonewall."

#313. "He is about five feet ten inches high, was eminently handsome in his youth, is still one of the finest looking men in the army, rides like a knight of the old crusading days, is indefatigable in business, and bears fatigue like a man of iron."
* A description of General Robert E. Lee. This text is from an 1864 booklet named *The War and Its Heroes* published in Richmond, Virginia.

#314. "You will, however, learn before this reaches you that our success at Gettysburg was not so great as reported--in fact, that we failed to drive the enemy from his position, and that our army withdrew to the Potomac. Had the river not unexpectedly risen, all would have been well with us; but God, in His all-wise providence, willed otherwise, and our communications have been interrupted and almost cut off."
* General Robert E. Lee writing to his family after his defeat at Gettysburg. This is from the book, *Recollections and Letters of General Robert E. Lee.*

#315. "You are the country to these men. They fought for you."
* Confederate General Henry Wise speaking to General Robert E. Lee at Appomattox Court House, Virginia before Lee's surrender in April 1865.

#316. "Aren't you ashamed to give Lee the privilege of being a President of a college? Satan wouldn't have him open the door for fresh arrivals, and you have pardoned him, and allowed him to take a position of the greatest responsibility. I hope you may have cause to repent that act in sackcloth and ashes. May the spirits of the dead heroes of America haunt you ever as a punishment for the cowardly neglect of duty."
* These words are from a letter written to President Andrew Johnson in

October 1865. President Johnson had made Robert E. Lee president of Washington College in Lexington, Virginia. Lee served in this position until his death on October 22, 1870. Lee was 64-years-old when he died and he is entombed at the college. The name of Washington College was later changed to Washington and Lee College.

#317. "There was nobody but soldiers on this train; but, if there had been women and children, too, it would have been all the same to me. Those who travel on a road running through a military district must accept the risk of the accidents of war. It does not hurt people any more to be killed in a railroad wreck than having their heads knocked off by a cannon shot."
* The thoughts of Confederate Major John Singleton Mosby after he torched a train in 1863.

#318.
"Who is that?" growled the sleepy brigadier.
"Get up quick, I want you," responded the major.
"Do you know who I am," cried the brigadier, sitting up in bed, with scowl. "I will have you arrested sir."
"Do you know who I am?" retorted the major, shortly.
"Who are you?"
"Did you ever hear of Mosby?"
"Yes! Tell me, have you caught the --- rascal?"
"No, but he has caught you!" And the major chuckled."
* In March 1863 Major John Singleton Mosby captured Union Brigadier General Edwin H. Stoughton. The story is that Stoughton was captured while sleeping and that Mosby snuck up and uncovered the sheets of the sleeping Stoughton, then slapped him on his rump.

#319.
"General Orders, No.—.

"Captain John S. Mosby has for a long time attracted the attention of his generals by his boldness, skill, and success, so signally displayed in his numerous forays upon the invaders of his native state. None know his daring enterprise and dashing heroism, better than those foul invaders, though strangers themselves to such noble traits.

"His late brilliant exploit—the capture of Brigadier General Stoughton, U. S. A., two captains, thirty other prisoners, together with their arms, equipments, and fifty-eight horses—justifies this recognition in the General Orders.

"This feat, unparalleled in the war, was performed in the midst of the enemy's troops, at Fairfax Court-House, without loss or injury.

"The gallant band of Captain Mosby share the glory, as they did the danger of this enterprise, and are worthy of such a leader.

"J.E.B. Stuart
Major General commanding"
* General J.E.B. Stuart's General Order praising Major John Singleton Mosby's capture of Union Brigadier General Edwin H. Stoughton in March 1863. Mosby had been a scout for J.E.B. Stuart.

#320. "When any of Mosby's men are caught, hang them without trial."
* General Ulysses S. Grant.

#321. "It became my painful duty, sir, to follow in the track of that charging column, and there, in a space not wider than the clerk's desk, and 300 yards long, lay the dead bodies of 543 of my colored comrades. fallen in the defense of their country, who had offered up their lives to uphold its flag and its honor as a willing sacrifice; and as I rode among them, guiding my horse this way and that way, lest he should profane with his hoof what seemed to me the sacred dead, and as I looked on their bronzed faces upturned in the shining sun to heaven, as if in mute appeal against the wrongs of the country for which they had given their lives, and whose flag had only been a flag of stripes, on which no stars of glory had ever shone for them—feeling I had wronged them in the past, and believing what was the future of my country to them—among my dead comrades there I swore to myself a solemn oath, "May my right hand forget its cunning and my tongue cleave to the roof of my mouth if I ever fail to defend the rights of these men who have given their blood for me and my country this day and for their race forever;" and, God helping me, I will keep that oath."
* General Benjamin Butler commanded the Army of the James, which

included a division of African-American troops, at Petersburg in 1864. Butler is speaking of the respect and honor he held for the dead African-American soldiers he encountered near the James River after Petersburg. Butler spoke these words in a speech in the House of Representatives after the Civil War.

#322.

General Order   HEADQUARTERS DEPARTMENT OF
THE GULF
No. 28   New Orleans, May 15, 1862.

As the officers and soldiers of the United States have been subject to repeated insults from the women (calling themselves ladies) of New Orleans, in return for the most scrupulous non-interference and courtesy on our part, it is ordered that hereafter when any female shall by word, gesture, or movement, insult or show contempt for any officer or soldier of the United States, she shall be regarded and held liable to be treated as a woman of the town plying her trade.

By command of Major-General Butler.

GEO. C. Stong; A.A. Gen. Chief of Staff
* General Benjamin Butler's General Orders No. 28 which became known as the "Woman Order." Some of the insults to the officers and soldiers of the United States made by the ladies of New Orleans included spitting on them, making offensive comments, and avoiding being near them by crossing a street or by leaving a room. A lady of New Orleans dumped the contents of a chamberpot on Navy Captain David Farragut after he'd taken control of the city.

#323.

B rutal and vulgar, a coward and knave;

F amed for no action, noble or brave;

B eastly by instinct, a tyrant and sot,

U gly and venomous-on mankind a blot--

T hief, liar, and scoundrel, in highest degree,

L et Yankeedom boast of such heroes as thee!

E very woman and child will for ages to come

R emember thee, monster--thou vilest of scum!

* A Confederate soldier's words and opinion of Union General Benjamin F. Butler. Note that "BFBUTLER" is spelled out vertically by the first letter of each line.

#324. "He will regret it but once, and that will be continually."
* Confederate General J.E.B. Stuart regarding his father-in-law General Philip St. George Cooke's choice to remain in the Union army. Stuart wrote this in a letter to his Confederate officer brother-in-law, John R. Cooke.

#325. "Not a great man except morally; not an original or brilliant man, but sincere, thoughtful, deep, and gifted with courage that never faltered."
* Charles Anderson Dana describing General Ulysses S. Grant. Dana was Assistant Secretary of War in 1863-1864.

#326. "Grant is played out with me [h]e were strong enough to drive the rebels if we wer managed right, but no he would bring us up in a Single line when the rebels were 6 or 8 deep and any fool would know we could not stand then."
* The opinion of a Union private named Thomas N. Lewis regarding Ulysses S. Grant's generalship at the Battle of Shiloh, April 6-7, 1862. Shiloh was the first large battle of the war and the number of killed was high. The word Shiloh means "place of peace."

#327. "General Grant, entrusted with our greatest army, is a jackass in the original package. He is a poor drunken imbecile. He is a poor stick sober, and he is most of the time more than half-drunk, and much of the time idiotically drunk...Grant will fail miserably, hopelessly, eternally."

* A letter from Marat Halstead, the editor of the *Cincinnati Commercial*, to United States Secretary of the Treasury Salmon P. Chase. Despite Halstead's misgivings about him, Ulysses S. Grant would become a great Union military leader in the Civil War and serve two terms as president.

#328. "By the way, can you tell me where he gets his whiskey? He has given us successes and if his whiskey does it, I should like to send a barrel of the same brand to every general in the field."
* President Abraham Lincoln regarding General Ulysses S. Grant's battle success and rumored drinking.

#329. "Grant is my man, and I am his the rest of the war!"
* President Abraham Lincoln after General Ulysses S. Grant captured Vicksburg on July 4, 1863.

#330. "If he had a million men he would swear the enemy has two millions, and then he would sit down in the mud and yell for three."
* United States Secretary of War Edwin M. Stanton commenting on General George Brinton McClellan. McClellan often overestimated the number of enemy forces opposing him and always believed that he needed more men and more supplies before he could take offensive action.

#331. "It is called the Army of the Potomac, but it is only McClellan's bodyguard...If McClellan is not using the army, I should like to borrow it for a while."
* President Abraham Lincoln, April 9, 1862, regarding General George B. McClellan. McClellan tested Lincoln's patience with his failure to take action against the rebels. This quote is from a note that Lincoln decided not to send.

#332. "General McClellan, if I understand you correctly, before you strike at the Rebels, you want to be sure of plenty of room so you can run in case they strike back."
* This is from Zachariah Chandler, a member of the Joint Committee on the Conduct of the War as he was questioning General George B. McClellan

regarding McClellan's inability to take offensive movement against the enemy.

#333. "McClellan's vice...was always waiting to have everything just as he wanted before he would attack, and before he could get things arranged as he wanted them, the enemy pounced on him."
* General George G. Meade's opinion of General George B. McClellan. McClellan was an excellent organizer and administrator who had a good strategic sense. His organizational skills as a commander were badly needed to prepare the army for war.

#334. "The effect of this man's presence upon the Army of the Potomac--in sunshine or in rain, in darkness or in daylight, in victory or defeat--was electrical, and too wonderful to make it worthwhile attempting to give a reason for it."
* Union General George B. McClellan's troops loved him. McClellan would hold grand reviews that would charge the morale of his men. This quote is from an anonymous soldier under McClellan's command.

#335. "He went beyond the formal military salute, and gave his cap a little twirl, which with his bow and smile seemed to carry a little personal good fellow-ship to the humblest private soldier...It was very plain that these little attentions to the troops took well, and had no small influence in establishing a sort of comradeship between him and them."
* A description of General George B. McClellan by an officer. McClellan's men thought he was the one who would bring them victory, they held him in awe and admiration.

#336. "He has got an eye like a hawk. I looked him right in the eye and he done the same by me."
* A Massachusetts soldier's impression of General George B. McClellan. McClellan was not tall in stature (around 5' 4") and was affectionately called "Little Mac" by the soldiers of the Army of the Potomac, the press called him "Young Napoleon."

#337. "Well, I've been tried and condemned without a hearing, and I suppose I shall have to go to execution."
* The words of Union General George Gordon Meade on June 27, 1863, when he learned that he was now in command of the Army of the Potomac. Meade would soon lead the Army of the Potomac at the Battle of Gettysburg to be fought on July 1-3, 1863. Previously, George B. McClellan, Ambrose Burnside, and Joseph Hooker had tried their luck at being commander of the Army of the Potomac. All of them had failed, Meade would not fail at Gettysburg.

#338. "General Sheridan, when this peculiar war began I thought a cavalryman should be at least six feet four high, but I have changed my mind. Five feet four will do in a pinch."
* President Abraham Lincoln to Philip Henry Sheridan. Sheridan had led a successful cavalry raid into northern Virginia in March 1865, and he would become one of the Union's top soldiers. As indicated in this Lincoln quote, Sheridan was short in stature (around 5' 5"). Sheridan was known as "Little Phil."

#339. "The Government of the United States may now safely proceed on the proper Rule that all in the South are enemies of all in the North; and not only are they unfriendly, but all who can procure arms now bear them as organized Regiments or as Guerillas."
* General William Tecumseh Sherman writing to Secretary of the Treasury Salmon P. Chase in August 1862.

#340. "Once let the black man get upon his person the brass letters, U.S., let him get an eagle on his button, and a musket on his shoulder and bullets in his pocket, and there is no power on earth which can deny that he has earned the right to citizenship in the United States."
* Abolitionist and freed slave Frederick Douglass, 1863.

#341. "Facts are beginning to dispel prejudices. Enemies of the negro race, who have persistently denied the capacity and doubted the courage of the Blacks, are unanswerably confuted by the good conduct and gallant deeds of the men whom they persecuted and slander."

* The *New York Tribune* newspaper, March 28, 1863.

#342. "You say you will not fight to free negroes. Some of them seem willing to fight for you. [When victory is won] there will be some black men who can remember that, with a silent tongue and clenched teeth, and steady eye and well-poised bayonet, they have helped mankind on to this great consummation; while, I fear, there will be some white ones, unable to forget that with a malignant heart and deceitful speech, they strove to hinder it."
* From a public letter by President Abraham Lincoln in August 1863 to those who opposed emancipation and the use of African-American troops in the war effort.

#343. "I know they says dese tings but dey is lies. Our masters may talk now all dey choose; but one tings sartin,-- dey don't dare to try us. Jess put de guns into our hans, and you'll soon see dat we not only knows how to shoot, but who to shoot. My master wouldn't be wuff much ef I was a soldier."
* These words are from a Virginia slave known only as Tom. Tom was offering his opposing opinion of the commonly held belief by slaveholders that the slaves loved their masters too much to choose to take up arms and fight against them. It seems that if slave Tom became a soldier, then Tom's master would be rudely surprised with Tom's actions toward him.

#344. "Our Presidents, Governors, Generals and Secretaries are calling, with almost frantic vehemence, for men.—"Men! men! send us men!" they scream, or the cause of the Union is gone; ...and yet these very officers, representing the people and the Government, steadily and persistently refuse to receive the very class of men which have a deeper interest in the defeat and humiliation of the rebels, than all others... What a spectacle of blind, unreasoning prejudice and pusillanimity this is! The national edifice is on fire. Every man who can carry a bucket of water, or remove a brick, is wanted; but those who have the care of the building, having a profound respect for the feeling of the national burglars who set the building on fire, are determined that the flames shall only be extinguished by Indo-Caucasian hands, and to have the building burnt rather than save it by means of any other. Such is the pride, the stupid prejudice and folly that

rules the hour."
* Abolitionist and freed slave Frederick Douglass in September 1861, regarding the Union not enlisting African-Americans to fight in the Civil War.

#345. "The bare sight of 50,000 armed and drilled black soldiers upon the banks of the Mississippi would end the rebellion at once."
* President Abraham Lincoln from a letter to Andrew Johnson, the military governor of Tennessee, on March 26, 1863. Lincoln liked Johnson's idea of raising an African-American military force.

#346. "I have given the subject of arming the Negro my hearty support. This, with the emancipation of the Negro, is the heaviest blow yet given the Confederacy....By arming the Negro we have added a powerful ally. They will make us good soldiers and taking them from the enemy weakens him in the same proportion they strengthen us."
* General Ulysses S. Grant.

#347. "This charge was resisted by the negro portion of the enemy's force with considerable obstinacy, while the white or true Yankee portion ran like whipped curs almost as soon as the charge was ordered."
* Confederate General Henry McCulloch. His comments regarding the performance of Union African-American troops at the attack on Milliken's Bend in June 1863.

#348. "I want you to prove yourselves. The eyes of thousands will look on what you do tonight."
* Union Colonel Robert Gould Shaw to his African-American regiment, the 54th Massachusetts Colored Infantry, before their assault on Fort Wagner, South Carolina on July 18, 1863. This regiment suffered heavy casualties in the attack and Colonel Shaw was killed. The 54th Massachusetts Colored Infantry performed their duty and fought with bravery and honor at Fort Wagner.

Frederick Douglass

#349. "Here the flag of this regiment was planted; here General Strong fell mortally wounded; and here the brave, beautiful, and heroic Colonel Shaw was saluted by death and kissed by immortality. The regiment lost heavily, but held its ground under the most discouraging circumstances."
* These words from an African-American historian named George Washington Williams in 1888. Williams is referring to the assault on Fort Wagner, South Carolina on July 18, 1863, by the 54th Massachusetts Colored Infantry.

#350. "The old flag never touched the ground."
* Sergeant William H. Carney was one of the members of the 54th Massachusetts Colored Infantry when it assaulted Fort Wagner, South Carolina. When the color bearer fell, and when an order to withdraw was given, Carney took hold of the regimental colors and returned them to his line despite being hit by rebel fire. Sergeant Carney was the first African-American to win a Congressional Medal of Honor.

#351. "The next day the 31st several flags of truce were sent from our lines proposing to recover the wounded and bury the dead, the rebels would not allow us to take the wounded negroes who laid strewn over the field [and] constituted the greater part of those who had fallen between the respective Forts of the opposing parties. The whites they allowed us to take."
* Samuel Rodman Smith was a member of the 4th Delaware Regiment. He is writing home to his mother after the Battle of the Crater, fought on July 30, 1864, at Petersburg.

#352.
Order by the President

Executive Mansion, Washington D.C July 30. 1863

It is the duty of every government to give protection to its citizens, of whatever class, color, or condition, and especially to those who are duly organized as soldiers in the public service. The law of nations and the usages and customs of war as carried on by civilized powers, permit no distinction as to color in the treatment of prisoners of war as public enemies. To sell or enslave any captured person, on account of his color, and for no offence against the laws of war, is a relapse into barbarism and a crime against the civilization of the age.

The government of the United States will give the same protection to all its soldiers, and if the enemy shall sell or enslave anyone because of his color, the offense shall be punished by retaliation upon the enemy's prisoners in our possession.

It is therefore ordered that for every soldier of the United States killed in violation of the laws of war, a rebel soldier shall be executed; and for every one enslaved by the enemy or sold into slavery, a rebel soldier shall be placed at hard labor on the public works and continued at such labor until the other shall be released and receive the treatment due to a prisoner of war

ABRAHAM LINCOLN

* This is President Abraham Lincoln's Order of Retaliation. July 30, 1863.

#353. "We don't know any black men here, they're all soldiers."
* From a white Union soldier after the assault on Fort Wagner, South Carolina by the 54th Massachusetts Colored Infantry on July 18, 1863.

#354.
Cairo Illinois

August 23d 1863.

Sir:

Your letter of the 9th inst. reached me at Vicksburg just as I was about starting for this place. Your letter of the 13th of July was also duly received.

After the fall of Vicksburg I did incline very much to an immediate move on Mobile. I believed then the place could be taken with but little effort, and with the rivers debouching there, in our possession, we would have such a base to opperate from on the very center of the Confederacy as would make them abandon entirely the states bound West by the Miss. I see however the importance of a movement into Texas just at this time.

I have reinforced Gen. Banks with the 13th Army corps comprising ten Brigades of Infantry with a full proportion of Artillery.

I have given the subject of arming the negro my hearty support. This, with the emancipation of the negro, is the heavyest blow yet given the Confederacy. The South care a great deal about it and profess to be very angry. But they were united in their action before and with the negro under subjection could spare their entire white population for the field. Now they complain that nothing can be got out of their negroes.

There has been great difficulty in getting able bodied negroes to fill up the colored regiments in consequence of the rebel cavalry running off all that class to Georgia and Texas. This is especially the case for a distance of fifteen or twenty miles on each side of the river. I am now however sending two expeditions into Louisiana, one from Natchez to Harrisonburg and one from Goodrich's Landing to Monroe, that I expect will bring back a large number. I have ordered recruiting officers to accompany these expeditions. I am also moving a Brigade of Cavalry from Tennessee to Vicksburg which will enable me to move troops to a greater distance into the interior and will facilitate materially the recruiting service.

Gen. Thomas is now with me and you may rely on it I will give him all the aid in my power. I would do this whether the arming the negro seemed to me a wise policy or not, because it is an order that I am bound to obey and do not feel that in my position I have a right to question any policy of the Government. In this particular instance there is no objection however to my expressing an honest conviction. That is, by arming the negro we have added a powerful ally. They will make good soldiers and taking them from the enemy weaken him in the same proportion they strengthen us. I am therefore most decidedly in favor of pushing this policy to the enlistment of a force sufficient to hold all the South falling into our hands and to aid in capturing more.

Thanking you very kindly for the great favors you have ever shown me I remain, very truly and respectfully

your obt. svt.

U. S. Grant

Maj. Gen.
* General Ulysses S. Grant's letter to Abraham Lincoln regarding the enlistment of African-American troops to fight for the Union.

#355. "This year has brought about many changes that at the beginning were or would have been thought impossible. The close of the year finds me a soldier for the cause of my race. May God bless the cause, and enable me in the coming year, to forward it on."
* An African-American Union soldier named Christopher Fleetwood recorded these words in his diary in December 1863. Fleetwood received the Medal of Honor for taking up the national colors after two color bearers had fallen during fighting at Chapin's Farm near Richmond, Virginia in 1864.

#356. "I would sooner stay here...than have our Government accede to their demands in regard to the negro soldier... Anyone, whatever may be his color, who wears the blue of Uncle Sam is entitled to protection, even if thousands have to be sacrificed in protecting him."
* Union Captain James Daunt Derrickson was a prisoner of war. His words upon learning the Union had refused a prisoner exchange unless African-American prisoners of war were also treated as required by the rules of war.

#357. "General Forrest captured Fort Pillow and about six hundred the most of them was Negroes he didn't any of them prisoners killed every one of them I think that was the best thing he iver done in his life."
* A Confederate soldier on April 23, 1864, regarding the Fort Pillow, Tennessee massacre. The number of killed in this quote is exaggerated, approximately 231 were killed. The Committee on the Conduct of the War concluded the rebels were guilty of murdering most of the Union garrison at Fort Pillow after they had surrendered. Although this conclusion has been debated by some historians, there is strong evidence the massacre is fact.

#358. "Damn you, you are fighting against your master."
* A Confederate soldier to a black Union private before he shot the private

in the mouth and threw him into a river during the Fort Pillow Massacre. The black private was named George Shaw and he lived to testify to a congressional committee investigating the Fort Pillow Massacre.

#359.
"Question. Were you there at the fight?
Answer. Yes, sir.
Question. When were you shot?
Answer. About four o'clock in the evening.
Question. After you had surrendered?
Answer. Yes, sir.
Question. Where were you at the time?
Answer. About ten feet from the river bank.
Question. Who shot you.
Answer. A rebel soldier."
* An excerpt from African-American Union private George Shaw's testimony to a congressional committee investigating the Fort Pillow Massacre. The Fort Pillow Massacre happened on April 12, 1864, when Confederate troops under Nathan Bedford Forrest killed Union African-American soldiers instead of taking them as prisoners of war. Fort Pillow was in Tennessee, it overlooked the Mississippi River.

#360.
"Question. How near did he come to you?
Answer. About ten feet.
Question. What did he say to you?
Answer. He said, "Damn you, what are you doing here?" I said, "Please don't shoot me." He said, "Damn you, you are fighting against your master." He raised his gun and fired, and the bullet went into my mouth and out the back part of my head. They threw me into the river, and I swam around and hung on there in the water until night."
* An excerpt from African-American Union private George Shaw's testimony to a congressional committee investigating the Fort Pillow Massacre.

#361.
"Question. Did you see anybody else shot?

Answer. Yes, sir; three young boys, lying in the water, with their heads out; they could not swim. They begged them as long as they could, but they shot them right in the forehead.

Question. How near to them were they?

Answer. As close as that stone, (about eight or ten feet.)

Question. How old were the boys?

Answer. Not more than fifteen or sixteen years old. They were not soldiers, but contraband boys, helping us on the breastworks."

* An excerpt from African-American Union private George Shaw's testimony to a congressional committee investigating the Fort Pillow Massacre.

#362. "The river was dyed with the blood of the slaughtered for 200 yards. It is hoped that these facts will demonstrate to the northern people that negro soldiers cannot cope with Southerners."

* Confederate General Nathan Bedford Forrest's comments after the Fort Pillow Massacre. After the Civil War, Forrest returned to planting and was involved with railroading. Nathan Bedford Forrest was also connected with the KKK, there is evidence he was a Grand Wizard.

#363. "When I was home I used to run down the colored troops as bad as any one, but one month in Virginia has entirely cured me of that as they did all the fighting in our corps and fought well."

* Soldier George C. Chandler of New Jersey explaining his change of attitude about African-American troops fighting in the Civil War.

#364. "When there is no officer with us, we take no prisoners."

* Union troops had their ways of taking revenge for the Fort Pillow Massacre.

#365.

"We have done with hoeing cotton, we have done with hoeing corn,
We are colored Yankee soldiers, now, as sure as you are born;
When the masters hear us yelling, they'll think it's Gabriel's horn,
As we go marching on..."

* This is the "Marching Song of the First Arkansas (Negro) Regiment" and

it is sung to the tune of the "Battle Hymn of the Republic."

#366. "The change seems almost miraculous. The very people who, three years ago, crouched at their master's feet, on the accursed soil of Virginia, now march in a victorious column of freedmen, over the same land."
* An African-American Union sergeant after marching into Richmond, Virginia in April 1865. General Robert E. Lee had surrendered to General Ulysses S. Grant at Appomattox Court House on April 9, 1865.

#367. "The army is constantly depleted by company officers who give their men leave of absence in the very face of the enemy, and on the very eve of an engagement, which is almost as bad as desertion. At this very moment there are between seventy and one hundred thousand men absent on furlough from the Army of the Potomac."
* President Abraham Lincoln, November 1862.

#368. "The army, like the nation, has become demoralized by the idea that the war is to be ended, the nation united, and peace restored, by strategy, and not by hard desperate fighting. Why, then, should not the soldiers have furloughs."
* President Abraham Lincoln, November 1862.

#369. "The courage with which you, in an open field, maintained the contest against an entrenched foe, and the consummate skill and success with which you crossed and re-crossed the river, in the face of the enemy, show that you possess all the qualities of a great army, which will yet give victory to the cause of the country and of popular government."
* President Abraham Lincoln, December 1862. The Union army had lost the Battle of Fredericksburg and this was Lincoln's message to his army. In early July 1863, the Union army had significant victories at Vicksburg and Gettysburg.

#370. "I can make more brigadier generals, but I can't make more horses."
* President Abraham Lincoln after learning that General Stoughton, 32 Union officers, and 58 Union horses had been captured by Confederate

Major John Singleton Mosby. March 1863.

#371. "You cannot conduct warfare against savages unless you become half savage yourself. ...I would practice every mode of warfare that is prescribed in either ancient or modern history."
* The thoughts of Ohio Senator John Sherman.

#372. "Our people are opposed to work. Our troops, officers, community, and press all ridicule and resist it. It is the very means by which McClellan has and is advancing. Why should we leave to him the whole advantage of labor. Combined with valour, fortitude & boldness, of which we have our fair proportion, it should lead us to success. What carried the Roman soldiers into all Countries but that happy combination? There is nothing so military as labor, and nothing so important to an army as to save the lives of its soldiers."
* General Robert E. Lee writing on June 5, 1862, from his headquarters near Richmond to Confederate President Jefferson Davis. The astute reader will note that the South preferred to use slaves as its labor source, while instead here Lee is promoting the use of elbow grease provided by the military.

#373. "This was the horrible episode of civil war to me, and although I had many relatives and hosts of friends serving under the Confederate flag all the time, I never fully realized the fratricidal character of the conflict until I lost my idolized brother Dave of the Southern army one day, and was nursing my Northern husband back to life the next."
* Words of a Union officer's wife.

#374. "We are not only fighting hostile armies, but a hostile people, and must make old and young, rich and poor, feel the hand of war."
* General William Tecumseh Sherman, from his book, *Memoirs of General W. T. Sherman*. Sherman lived up to this quote during his 1864 March to the Sea.

#375. "The necessities of state require that all the inhabitants of a hostile

country should be treated as enemies whether in arms or not. Even women and children are enemies, and are to be treated as such in every respect, except when dealing with them personally. There can be no neutrals in a hostile country....The humanity of modern civilization does not justify putting them to death, unless absolutely necessary. Foreigners residing in a hostile country are enemies, and their property is as much subject to seizure as that of natives. Being non combatants makes no difference, except in dealing with their lives. These extreme rights of war between nations are intensified when one of the belligerents happens to consist of traitors."
* Pennsylvania Congressman Thaddeus Stevens. Stevens strongly believed in abolition. He also was chairman of the Ways and Means committee and had a large amount of influence on the war and the country.

#376. "No one could say at any hour that he would be living the next. Men were killed in their camps, at their meals, and... in their sleep. So many men were daily struck in the camp and about with little concern, dodging around a corner when they heard a shell coming, or putting their heads out of their windows to see damage they had done. ...A lady yesterday sent Wardlaw and myself some ice cream and cakes."
* The memories of a Union veteran who fought at Petersburg.

#377. "We must make this campaign an exceedingly active one. Only thus can a weaker country cope with a stronger. It must make up in activity what it lacks in strength, and a defensive campaign can only be made successful by taking the aggression at the proper time. Don't wait for the adversary to become fully prepared, but strike him the first blow."
* General Thomas Jonathan "Stonewall" Jackson before Chancellorsville, 1863.

#378. "In one word, I would not take any risk of being entangled upon the river, like an ox jumped half over a fence, and liable to be torn by dogs, front and rear, without a fair chance to gore one way or kick the other."
* President Abraham Lincoln offering colorful advice to General Joseph "Fighting Joe" Hooker in a June 5, 1863, letter. Lincoln is discussing how Hooker might best handle Robert E. Lee at the Rappahannock River after Hooker's defeat at Chancellorsville. The Battle of Chancellorsville is known

as Lee's Masterpiece.

#379. "Oh, I am heartily tired of hearing what Lee is going to do. Some of you always seem to think he is suddenly going to turn a double somersault, and land on our rear and on both our flanks at the same time. Go back to your command, and try to think what we are going to do ourselves, instead of what Lee is going to do."
* General Ulysses S. Grant during the Overland Campaign (Wilderness Campaign), May 5-7, 1864.

#380.
Executive Mansion, Washington, July 13, 1863.

My Dear General: I do not remember that you and I ever met personally. I write this now as a grateful acknowledgment for the almost inestimable service you have done the country. I wish to say a word further. When you first reached the vicinity of Vicksburg, I thought you should do, what you finally did--march the troops across the neck, run the batteries with the transports, and thus go below; and I never had any faith, except a general hope that you knew better than I, that the Yazoo Pass expedition, and the like, could succeed. When you got below, and took Port-Gibson, Grand Gulf, and vicinity, I thought you should go down the river and join Gen. Banks; and when you turned Northward East of the Big Black, I feared it was a mistake. I now wish to make the personal acknowledgment that you were right, and I was wrong.
Yours very truly
A. Lincoln
* President Abraham Lincoln's letter to General Ulysses S. Grant regarding the Vicksburg Campaign. Vicksburg was taken by Grant on July 4, 1863, only a day after the Union victory at Gettysburg.

#381. "If the Vicksburg campaign meant anything, in a military point of view, it was that there are no fixed laws of war which are not subject to the conditions of the country, the climate, and the habits of the people."
* Ulysses S. Grant after the Civil War.

#382.
"General Pickett rode to confer with Alexander, then to the ground upon which I was resting, where he was soon handed a slip of paper. After reading it he handed it to me. It read:

"If you are coming at all, come at once, or I cannot give you proper support, but the enemy's fire has not slackened at all. At least eighteen guns are still firing from the cemetery itself.
Alexander.

"Pickett said, 'General, shall I advance?

"The effort to speak the order failed, and I could only indicate it by an affirmative bow. He accepted the duty with seeming confidence of success, leaped on his horse, and rode gayly to his command."
* General James Longstreet describing events before Pickett's Charge at the Battle of Gettysburg on July 3, 1863. Edward Porter Alexander commanded Longstreet's artillery.

#383. "Three years ago by a little reflection and patience they could have had a hundred years of Peace & Prosperity, but they preferred War. Last year they could have saved their Slaves, but now it is too late, All the Powers of Earth cannot restore to them their any more than their dead Grandfathers. Next year in all probability their lands will be taken, for in War we can take them & rightfully too, and in another year they may beg in vain for their lives, for sooner or later there must be an end to strife."
* General William Tecumseh Sherman in January 1864 regarding the situation of the Confederates. Lee surrendered to Grant on April 9, 1865. Thankfully, the Civil War ended before the time estimate Sherman makes in this quote.

#384. "By the time we reached Cold Harbor we had begun to understand what our new adversary meant, and therefore, for the first time, I think, the men in the ranks of the Army of Northern Virginia realized that the era of experimental campaigns against us was over; that Grant was not going to retreat; that he was not to be removed from command because he had failed to break Lee's resistance; and that the policy of pounding had begun, and would continue until our strength be utterly worn away, unless by some

decisive blow to the army in our front, or some brilliant movement in diversion we should succeed in changing the character of the contest. We began to understand that Grant had taken hold of the problem of destroying the Confederate strength in the only way that the strength of such an army, so commanded, could be destroyed, and that he intended to continue the plodding work till the task should be accomplished, wasting very little time or strength in efforts to make a brilliant display of generalship in a contest of strategic wits with Lee. We at last began to understand what Grant had meant by his expression of determination to fight it out on this line if it takes all summer."
* Sergeant George Cary Eggleston at Cold Harbor on June 1, 1864, speaking of what he believed the Confederates could expect of General Ulysses S. Grant. General Robert E. Lee won at Cold Harbor and Union casualties were heavy

#385. "They began the war with a contempt for the spade, but now thoroughly believe in it. They use bayonets, tin pans, and even, I am told, split their tin canteens to get a utensil that will throw up earth."
* Josiah Gorgas was Chief of Ordnance for the Confederate army. He is remarking here how the Confederate troops learned to appreciate how valuable it was to have breastworks fortifying their lines. After the Civil War, Gorgas was the president and then the librarian, of the University of Alabama.

#386.
"Gen. Sheridan says:
'If the thing is pressed I think Lee will surrender.'
Let the thing be pressed."
* President Abraham Lincoln, from a telegram to General Ulysses S. Grant on April 7, 1865, while Grant was at City Point, Virginia. Grant pressed. On April 9, 1865, Lee surrendered to Grant at Appomattox Court House, Virginia.

#387. "This is a sad business, Colonel. ...It has happened as I told them in Richmond it would happen. The line has been stretched until it is broken."
* General Robert E. Lee to an aide as they rode toward Petersburg on April 2, 1865. Robert E. Lee and his Army of Northern Virginia were running out

of time.

#388. "Have we not, as a people, been more forebearing than any people on earth? Did we not bear the taunts and insults of these secessionists until forbearance was cowardice? Have they not tried to coerce you into rebellion and did they not begin to burn the houses of Union men in Kentucky, when I, poor innocent, would not let a soldier take a green apple or a fence rail to make a cup of coffee? Why! we have not yet caught up with our friends in the South in this respect for private rights. ...I pledge my honor when the South ceases its strife, sends members to Congress, and appeals to the courts for its remedy and not to 'horrid war,' I will be the open advocate for mercy and restoration to home, and peace, and happiness of all who have lost them by my acts."
* General William Tecumseh Sherman to the governor of Kentucky regarding the restraint of his soldiers in Kentucky in 1861. The governor complained to Sherman about martial law in Kentucky and Sherman scolded him. At the time, secessionists were burning homes of those who supported the Union. During Sherman's March to the Sea in 1864, there was ample plunder and pillage made by the soldiers in blue.

#389. "No goths or vandals ever had less respect for the lives and property of friends and foes, and henceforth we ought never to hope for any friends in Virginia."
* General William Tecumseh Sherman was angry with his troops who pillaged in Virginia. Summer, 1861.

#390. "The country seems possessed by demons, black and white."
* The words of Kate Stone as her Louisiana plantation was being plundered.

#391. "Get there first with the most men."
* The brief war strategy of Confederate General Nathan Bedford Forrest. The veracity of this quote is sometimes questioned. This quote has this version too, "Get there firstest with the mostest."

120

#392. "That devil Forrest must be hunted down and killed if it costs ten thousand lives and bankrupts the Federal treasury."
* General William Tecumseh Sherman regarding Nathan Bedford Forrest. Forrest was causing Sherman trouble in the summer and fall of 1864.

#393.
GEO. C. STRONG, A. A. G., Chief of Staff
Men of the South! shall our mothers, our wives, our daughters, and our sisters, be thus outraged by the ruffianly soldiers of the North, to whom it is given the right to treat, at their pleasure, the ladies of the South as common harlots? Arouse friends, and drive back from our soil, those infamous invaders of our homes and disturbers of our family ties.

(Signed,)

G. T. BEAUREGARD, General Commanding.
* General Orders No. 44 from Pierre Gustave Toutant Beauregard on May 19, 1862. Beauregard is responding to General Benjamin Butler's General Orders, No. 28. which can be found here as Quote and Note #322.

#394. "Boys, do you hear that musketry and that artillery? It means that our friends are falling by the hundreds at the hands of the enemy, and here we are guarding a damned creek! Let's go and help them. What do you say?"
* General Nathan Bedford Forrest to his men at Shiloh.

#395. "As I have intimated, the orders from General Lee for the protection of private property and persons were of the most stringent character. Guided by these instructions and my own impulses, I resolved to leave no ruins along the line of my march through Pennsylvania; no marks of a more enduring character than the tracks of my soldiers along its superb pikes."
* Confederate General John B. Gordon, June 1863. The campaign was underway that would culminate with the Confederate defeat at Gettysburg.

#396. "Like bees going to a Hive, the Boys one after another would crowd on to the Porch, into the Hall, Parlor, Kitchen or Bedroom, appropriating every thing useful or ornamental which they thought they could take care of."

* A Union soldier commenting on plunder by the army.

#397. "A crow flying over the valley would have to carry his own provisions."

* General Phil Sheridan regarding the plunder of the Shenandoah Valley by his troops during the winter of 1864. The Shenandoah Valley was a source of food and fodder and a natural route of invasion into the North for the Confederacy. Much conflict would take place during the Civil War in the beautiful country of the Shenandoah Valley.

#398. "Abe Linkhorn, We received your proklamation, and as you have put us on very short notis, a few of us boys have conkluded to write you, and ax for a little more time. The fact is, we are most obleeged to have a few more days, for the way things are happening, it is utterly onpossible for us to disperse in twenty days. I tried my darndest yisterday to disperse and retire, but it was no go."

* Bill Arp. When Fort Sumter was fired upon, President Abraham Lincoln put out a proclamation asking the rebels to "disperse and retire." The above is a letter to Lincoln that appeared in a newspaper. "Bill Arp" is the pen name of humorist Charles Henry Smith.

#399. "I have travelled a heap of late, and had occasion to retire into some very sequestered regions, but nary a hill or holler, nary mountain gorge or inaccessible ravine have I found, but what the cavalry had been there, and just left. And that is the reason they can't be whipped, for they have always just left, and took an odd horse or two with'em."

* The Southern humorist Bill Arp regarding the Confederate cavalry.

Abraham Lincoln

#400. "A group of respectable New Yorkers tried to get their countrymen to write a national hymn that summer, and when the entries were submitted, found themselves the nation's largest collection of waste-paper. Four or five bales of made-to-order songs arrived in one afternoon; most of them could be described as the first wartime atrocities."
* These words by historian Mark Wahlgren Summers. The "Battle Hymn of the Republic" would become the rallying song for the North, but not through the efforts of these New Yorkers searching for a national hymn.

#401. "I have no word of encouragement to give! The fact is the people have not yet made up their minds that we are at war with the South. They have not buckled down to the determination to fight this war through; for they have got the idea into their heads that we are going to get out of this fix somehow by strategy! That's the word—strategy! General McClellan thinks he is going to whip the Rebels by strategy; and the army has got the same notion."
* President Abraham Lincoln to Mary Livermore, a member of the Sanitary Commission. This commission tried to elevate the hygienic conditions of the army camps, improve the diets of the soldiers, help the wounded, and perform other good acts of care to make the war more tolerable for the men in blue uniform. The Sanitary Commission attempted to do what the government could not or would not do. Livermore and other Sanitary Commission workers had called on President Lincoln hoping for words of encouragement from him regarding the war, but the president could not be encouraging.

#402. "The people are wild for peace."
* An observation by a New Yorker named Thurlow Weed when morale in the North was very low and some wanted the war to end, even if it meant allowing the Union to be broken. Weed didn't think Lincoln would be re-elected in 1864. Despite Weed's pessimism, military successes by Grant and Sherman helped Lincoln win a second term in the White House.

#403. "A dog fight, a scared horse, a smoking chimney, or a runaway negro, is all that is necessary to put the people in a stir."
* A report from Montgomery, Alabama during the Confederate Convention. This convention began on February 2, 1861, with Montgomery as the

original capital of the Confederacy. On May 20, 1861, the Confederate capital was moved to Richmond, Virginia where it remained until the conclusion of the Civil War.

#404. "War, war! is the one idea. The children play only with cannons and soldiers; the oldest inhabitant goes by every day with his rifle to practice; the public squares are full of companies drilling, and are now the fashionable resorts. We have been told that it is best for women to learn to shoot too, so as to protect themselves when the men have all gone to battle. Every evening after dinner we adjourn to the back lot and fire at a target with pistols."
* A woman known only as "G" who lived in New Orleans but supported the Union. This is a diary entry of hers from April 20, 1861.

#405. "I went to tell Ma & Pa. How I did hate to do it. Poor Pa & Ma. Pa got up. He has been walking the floor all day. He says his peace is broken forever on this earth. His only boy, his pride, the idol of Ma's heart."
* Confederate Bud Craighead was killed in the war. These words are his sister Rachel's, whose task it was to inform her parents of Bud's death. Before the Civil War ended, the total number of deaths would be over six hundred thousand (this number has been revised and it is now estimated to be approximately 750,000), or 2% of the population for both sides combined. Besides wounds, disease was also a major cause of death in the Civil War. Poor Ma. Poor Pa. Hey Rachel, how about poor Bud!

#406. "One woman demanded to see my authority to search her house...I pointed her to a line of soldiers standing in front of the house and told her there was my authority and the power to enforce it."
* A Union officer describing his discussion with a Confederate lady regarding his authority and power. We can probably safely assume the good lady understood the officer's explanation of his source of authority .

#407. "A pair of old coat sleeves saved-nothing is thrown away now--was in my trunk. I cut an exact pattern from my shoes, laid it on the sleeves, and cut out thus good uppers and sewed them carefully; then soaked the soles and sewed the cloth to them. I am so proud of these home-made shoes,

think I'll put them in a glass case when the war is over, as an heirloom."
* This is a diary entry from April 28, 1861, of the New Orleans woman known only as "G." She suffered the deprivations of war that made life so hard in the South. Even though it is still very early in the Civil War, here G seems to know of the scarcity of goods that will come, she knows not to waste anything. G was a wise lady.

#408. "I want all blankets and carpets that can possibly be spared. I want them, ladies of Alabama, to shield your noble defenders against an enemy more to be dreaded than the Northern foe with musket in hand--the snows of coming winter. Do you know that thousands of our heroic soldiers of the West sleep on cold, damp ground, without tents? Perhaps not. You enjoy warm houses and comfortable beds."
* This was asked of the Confederate women of Alabama by Captain W. M. Gillespie in October 1863. Winter was fast approaching and the rebel troops needed the means to stay warm. The ladies of Alabama were expected to sacrifice their blankets and carpets to the soldiers who would go through winter without warm houses and comfortable beds.

#409. "Aunty had been ordered to leave her beautiful home to give place to a Yankee colonel who had given her only half a day to move all her property. O cruel soldier! could you not be a little more lenient? Could you not allow her one day for this work?"
* Atlanta, Georgia was occupied by the Yankees in 1864. Occupation meant inconveniences for the citizens of Atlanta as the Yankees made themselves comfortable in the conquered land of the South. To the victor go the spoils.

#410. "Immediately is a quick word, gentlemen, to a man who has lived at a place 40 years."
* A Union supporter in Kentucky after being told by Johnny Rebs that he must immediately leave his house and home.

#411. "There they are cutting each other's throats, because one half of them prefer hiring servants for life, and the other by the hour."
* Thoughts regarding the Civil War by Thomas Carlyle, a 19th-century British historian. The reader will note that Carlyle here erroneously equates

the Southern institution of slavery to "hiring servants for life." Slaves were not hired. The slaves were owned. The slave owners profited from the labor of their slaves, they did not pay them. Slave owners forced their slaves to work by brutally keeping them in submission. Slaves remained slaves for life until they died, were freed, or fled North to freedom.

#412.
"To Fight for Uncle Abe"

Way down in old Virginie
I suppose you all do know
They have tried to bust the Union
But they find it is no go
The yankee boys are starting out
The Union for to save
And We're marching down to Washington
to fight for Uncle Abe.

(Chorus)

Rip Rap, Flip Flap
Strap your knapsacks on your back
For we're a gwaing to Washington
to fight for Uncle Abe

There is General Grant at Vicksburg
Just see what he has done
He has taken 60 cannon
and made the rebels run
And next he will take Richmond
I'll bet you half a dollar
And If he catches General Johnson
Oh won't he make him holler.

(Chorus)

The season now is coming
when the roads begin to dry.
Soon the army of Potomac

will make the rebels fly.
For General (MacClellen, Hooker,
Meade, Grant) he's the man
The Union for to save.
Oh Hail Columbia's right side up
and so's your Uncle Abe.

(Chorus)

You may talk of southern chivalry
and cotton being king.
But I guess before the war is done
you'll think another thing.
They say that recognition will
the rebel country save
But Johnny Bull and Mister France
are 'fraid of Uncle Abe.

(Chorus)
* A fight song of Union soldiers entitled "To Fight for Uncle Abe." There are other versions of the lyrics.

#413. "We may have our own opinions about slavery, we may be for or against the South; but there is no that Jefferson Davis and other leaders of the South have made an army; they are making, it appears, a navy; and they have made what is more than either--they have made a nation."
* The words of Chancellor of the Exchequer William Ewart Gladstone, a member of the British government.

#414. "The privileged classes all over Europe rejoice in the thoughts of the ruin of the great experiment in popular government."
* Charles Francis Adams. Adams was the United States Minister to the Court of St. James'. He was also the son of John Quincy Adams, the sixth President of The United States.

#415. "America, teacher of liberty to our Fathers, now opens the most solemn Era of human progress, and whilst she amazes the world by her

gigantic boldness, makes us sadly reflect that this old Europe albeit agitated by the grand cause of human freedom, does not understand, nor move forward to become equal to her."
* These words were written to President Abraham Lincoln by three Italian nationalists named G., M., and N. Garibaldi. They are referring to the Emancipation Proclamation which was issued by Lincoln on September 22, 1862, and then took effect on January 1, 1863.

#416. "There is certainly not one government in Europe but is watching the war in this country with the ardent prayer that the United States may be effectually split, crippled, and dismembered by it. There is not one but would help toward that dismemberment, if it dared. I say such is the ardent wish today of England and of France, and of all nations of Europe, as governments."
* Poet Walt Whitman, 1864.

#417. "The North, it has the largest purse."
* Baron Rothschild was a London banker. He gave this answer when asked who he thought would win the Civil War.

#418. "My duty is to obey orders."
* Confederate General Thomas Jonathan "Stonewall" Jackson.

#419. "the Colored man is like A lost sheep. Meney of them old and young was Brave and Active. But has been hurrided By ignominious Death into Eternity. But I hope God will Presearve the Rest Now in existance to Get Justice and Rights. we have to Do our Duty or Die and no help for us. It is true the Country is in A hard strugle. But we All must Remember Mercy and Justice Grate and small. it is Devine."
* The words and thoughts of an African-American soldier.

#420. "But let us honestly state the facts. Our America has a bad name for superficialness. Great men, great nations, have not been boasters and buffoons, but perceivers of the terror of life, and have manned themselves to face it."

* Ralph Waldo Emerson, 1860.

#421. "I used to think war was a science, but its a mistake....the great majority of battles are the result of axident. And the results are the results of axidents."
* A Union officer named Thomas Edwin Smith.

#422. "Wars are not all evil, they are part of the grand machinery by which this world is governed; thunder storms, which purify the political atmosphere, test the manhood of a people, and prove whether they are worthy to take rank with others engaged in the same task by different methods."
* General William Tecumseh Sherman after the Civil War.

#423. "I am not so much impressed as many respecting the invincibility of our volunteers and their determination to be free—they are good for a dash but fail in tenacity. I don't think we can yet regard ourselves as soldiers—our men are not sufficiently impressed with a sense of honor that it is better to die by fire than to run—we fail also in company officers, they want skill and instruction and lamentably neglect their duty."
* Confederate General William Hardee after the Battle of Shiloh. Shiloh was fought on April 6-7, 1862.

#424. "The dogmas of the quiet past, are inadequate to the stormy present. The occasion is piled high with difficulty, and we must rise with the occasion. As our case is new, so we must think anew, and act anew."
* Excerpt from President Abraham Lincoln's annual message to Congress made on December 1, 1862.

#425. "Sir, if you ever presume again to speak disrespectfully of General Grant in my presence, either you or I will sever his connection with this university."
* After the Civil War, Robert E. Lee became the president of Washington College in Lexington, Virginia. This was Lee's response to a fellow faculty member who had spoken poorly and insultingly of Ulysses S. Grant.

#426. "I, -- -- --, do solemnly swear, in presence of Almighty God, that I will henceforth faithfully support, protect, and defend the Constitution of the United States and the union of the states thereunder; and that I will, in like manner, abide by and faithfully support all acts of Congress passed during the existing rebellion with reference to slaves, so long and so far as not repealed, modified, or held void by Congress, or by decision of the Supreme Court; and that I will in like manner, abide by and faithfully support all proclamations made by the President during the existing rebellion having reference to slaves, so long and so far as not modified or declared void by decision of the Supreme Court. So help me God."
* Those who signed this Oath of Allegiance to the Union were pardoned for their rebellion.

#427. "On principle I dislike an oath which requires a man to swear he has not done wrong. It rejects the Christian principle of forgiveness on terms of repentance. I think it is enough if the man does no wrong hereafter."
* Comments of President Abraham Lincoln in a letter to Edwin M. Stanton, February 5, 1864, regarding the Oath of Allegiance.

#428. "I had rather our throats were all cut, or turned to beggars on the world than that Bro. John should disgrace himself by taking that dirty oath."
* The thoughts of Kate Carney of Murfreesboro, Tennessee regarding the oath required for pardon.

#429.
Sheridan at Cedar Creek

Shoe the steed with silver
    That bore him to the fray,
When he heard the guns at dawning—
        Miles away;
When he heard them calling, calling—
        Mount! nor stay:
            Quick, or all is lost;

They've surprised and stormed the post,
   They push your routed host—
Gallop! retrieve the day!

House the horse in ermine—
   For the foam-flake blew
White through the red October;
   He thundered into view;
They cheered him in the looming;
   Horseman and horse they knew.
      The turn of the tide began,
      The rally of bugles ran,
      He swung his hat in the van;
   The electric hoof-spark flew.

Wreathe the steed and lead him—
   For the charge he led
Touched and turned the cypress
   Into amaranths for the head
Of Philip, king of riders,
   Who raised them from the dead.
      The camp (at dawning lost)
      By eve recovered—forced,
      Rang with laughter of the host
   At belated Early fled.

Shroud the horse in sable—
   For the mounds they heap!
There is firing in the Valley,
   And yet no strife they keep;
It is the parting volley,
   It is the pathos deep.
      There is glory for the brave
      Who lead, and nobly save,
      But no knowledge in the grave
   Where the nameless followers sleep.
* The poem "Sheridan at Cedar Creek" by Herman Melville. October 1864.

#430. "Who is to blame for all this waste of human life? Is it too bad to talk about. And what does it amount to? Has there been anything gained by all this sacrifice? What were we fighting for, the principles of slavery?

"And now the slaves are all freed, and the Confederacy has to be dissolved. We have to go back into the Union. Ah! there is the point. Will there ever be any more Union, as there once was?"
* The thoughts of Confederate Captain Samuel T. Foster in April 1865. General Robert E. Lee had surrendered to General Grant at Appomattox Court House on April 9, 1865.

#431. "War is at best barbarism. ...Its glory is all moonshine. It is only those who have neither fired a shot, nor heard the shrieks and groans of the wounded who cry aloud for blood, more vengeance, more desolation. War is hell."
* From General William Tecumseh Sherman's June 19, 1879, commencement address to the Michigan Military Academy.

#432. "I did only what my duty demanded; I could have taken no other course without dishonor & if all was to be done over again, I should act precisely in the same manner."
* Former Confederate General Robert E. Lee, after the Civil War.

#433. "...a face nor child nor old, very calm, as of beautiful yellow-white ivory;
Young man I think I know you-- I think this is the face of the Christ himself,
Dead and divine and brother of all, and here again he lies."
* A verse from Walt Whitman's poem, "A Sight in Camp in the Daybreak Gray and Dim." Whitman wrote this poem after seeing bodies piled outside of a hospital tent.

#434. "O God I pray the[e] to Direct a bullet or a bayonet to pirce the Hart or every northern soldier that invade southern Soile...I all so ask the[e] to aide the Southern Confederacy in maintaining Ower rites & establishing the confederate Government."
* From a plantation overseer near New Orleans in June 1861.

#435. "My mistress was a dreadful pious woman. She would pray, ever so long in the morning, then come out and sit down in her rocking chair, with her cowhide and cut and slash everybody who passed her. ...Sometimes I was afraid she was not a Christian, but she was mighty pious."
* The words of a Virginia slave. The cowhide was a whip.

#436. "Why should Christians be at all disturbed about the dissolution of the Union? It can only come by God's permission, and will only be permitted, if for his people's good, for does he not say that all things shall work together for good to them that love God?"
* Confederate General Thomas Jonathan "Stonewall" Jackson.

#437.
"Mother! when around your child
You clasp your arms in love,
And when with grateful joy you raise
Your eyes to God above—
Think of the negro mother, When
Her child is torn away,
Sold for a little slave,--oh then
For that poor mother pray!"
* These words could be found written in ink or sewn into quilts sold at anti-slavery fairs.

#438. "My interference in battle would do more harm than good. I have, then, to rely on my brigade and division commanders. I think and work with all my power to bring the troops to the right place at the right time; then I have done my duty. As soon as I order them into battle, I leave my army in the hands of God."
* General Robert E. Lee.

#439. "I think that the damned old cuss of a Preacher lied like Dixie for he sayed that God has fought our battle and won our victorys. Now if he has done all that why is it not in the papers, and why has he not been promoted."

* Union Sergeant Albinus Fell of the 6th Ohio Cavalry. It is not known which "old cuss of a Preacher" he was referring to.

#440. "The rebels can afford to give up all their church bells, cow bells and dinner bells to Beauregard, for they never go to church now, their cows have all been taken by foraging parties, and they have no dinner to be summoned to."
* Confederate General Pierre Gustave Toutant Beauregard (the "Hero of Sumter"), made a request in 1862 to the citizens of Mississippi that they give their bells so they could be melted down and made into cannon for the Confederate cause. This quote appeared in the pro-Union *Louisville Courier*.

#441.
Headquarters Army No Va
August 13th 1863

General Orders No 83,

The President of the Confederate States has, in the name of the people, appointed the 21st day of August as a day of humiliation, fasting and prayer. A strict observance of the day is enjoined upon the officers and soldiers of this Army. All Military duties, except such as are absolutely necessary, will be suspended.

The Commanding Officers of Brigades and Regiments are requested to cause divine services suitable to the occasion to be performed in their respective commands.

Soldiers! We have sinned against Almighty God. We have forgotten His signal mercies and have cultivated a vengeful, haughty and boastful spirit. We have not remembered that the defenders of a just cause should be pure in His eyes; that our lives are in His hand and we have relied too much on our own arms for the achievement of our independence.

God is our only refuge and our strength. Let us humble ourselves before Him. Let us confess our many sins and beseech Him to give us a higher Courage, a purer patriotism and more determined will. That He will convert the hearts of our enemies; that He will hasten the time when war with its sorrows and sufferings shall cease, and that He will give us a name and peace among the Nations of the earth.

R E Lee
Genl
* After the Army of Northern Virginia's defeat at the Battle of Gettysburg,
General Robert E. Lee issued General Orders No. 83 to his troops on
August 13, 1863.

#442. "I want to be able to read the Bible before I die."
* An unknown man expressed his hopes at the John Tyler's school for
African-Americans in September 1861.

#443. "It seems like the Lord has turned his face from us and left us to
work out our destruction."
* A Confederate soldier from Georgia serving under General Joseph E.
Johnston as they faced the Union troops of General William Tecumseh
Sherman across the Chattahoochee River. July 6, 1864.

#444.
Executive Mansion,
Washington, September 4, 1864.

Eliza P. Gurney.
My esteemed friend.

I have not forgotten--probably never shall forget--the very impressive
occasion when yourself and friends visited me on a Sabbath forenoon two
years ago. Nor has your kind letter, written nearly a year later, ever been
forgotten. In all, it has been your purpose to strengthen my reliance on
God. I am much indebted to the good Christian people of the country for
their constant prayers and consolations; and to no one of them, more than
to yourself. The purposes of the Almighty are perfect, and must prevail,
though we erring mortals may fail to accurately perceive them in advance.
We hoped for a happy termination of this terrible war long before this; but
God knows best, and has ruled otherwise. We shall yet acknowledge His
wisdom and our own error therein. Meanwhile we must work earnestly in
the best light He gives us, trusting that so working still conduces to the

great ends He ordains. Surely He intends some great good to follow this mighty convulsion, which no mortal could make, and no mortal could stay.

Your people--the Friends--have had, and are having, a very great trial. On principle, and faith, opposed to both war and oppression, they can only practically oppose oppression by war. In this hard dilemma, some have chosen one horn, and some the other. For those appealing to me on conscientious grounds, I have done, and shall do, the best I could and can, in my own conscience, under my oath to the law. That you believe this I doubt not; and believing it, I shall still receive, for our country and myself, your earnest prayers to our Father in heaven.

Your sincere friend
A. Lincoln.
* President Abraham Lincoln's letter to Eliza Gurney. Gurney was the widow of Joseph J. Gurney, an English Quaker. Joseph Gurney was anti-slavery and anti-war. Two years previously, Eliza Gurney had visited Lincoln to tell him she was praying for him.

#445. "Certainly not; crackers and oats are more necessary to my army than any moral or religious authority."
* General William Tecumseh Sherman was preparing for his 1864 Atlanta campaign. He needed to keep the supply trains running in order to build up a supply of food and ammunition for his troops. Sherman excluded any passengers on the trains to make more room for supplies. However, members of the United States Christian Commission had applied for passes to travel by railroad to the front lines. This was Sherman's response.

#446. "Both read the same Bible and pray to the same God; and each invokes His aid against the other. It may seem strange that any men should dare to ask a just God's assistance in wringing their bread from the sweat of other men's faces; but let us not judge that we be not judged. The prayers of both could not be answered; that of neither has been answered fully."
* From President Abraham Lincoln's second Inaugural Address. March 4, 1865.

#447. "Fondly do we hope--fervently do we pray--that this mighty scourge

of war may speedily pass away. Yet, if God wills that it continue, until all the wealth piled by the bondman's two hundred and fifty years of unrequited toil shall be sunk, and until every drop of blood drawn with the lash, shall be paid with another drawn with the sword, as was said three thousand years ago, so still it must be said 'the judgments of the Lord, are true and righteous altogether.'"
* From President Abraham Lincoln's second Inaugural Address. March 4, 1865.

#448.
"Oh, Jesus tell you once before,
Babylon's fallin' to rise no more;
To go in peace an' sin no more;
Babylon's fallin' to rise no more."
* African-Americans sang this song when Richmond fell to the Yankees.

#449. "A soldier has a hard life and but little consideration."
* General Robert E. Lee knew Lewis Armistead when they were serving at Fort Riley in Kansas. Armistead had left the fort with his company while an epidemic was raging through the fort. When Armistead and his men were only thirty miles away from the fort, a courier came to them with the news that Armistead's wife had died during the epidemic. He returned to the fort that night, buried his wife the next morning, then took his two children with him back to the company's camp in the field. This was Lee's comment to his wife when he told her of what had happened to Armistead's family.

#450. "The world has never had a good definition of the word liberty, and the American people, just now, are much in want of one. We all declare for liberty; but in using the same word we do not all mean the same thing."
* An excerpt from an address President Abraham Lincoln gave on April 18, 1864, at Baltimore, Maryland.

A Billy Yank:
Pvt. Levi Miller, Ohio Regiment, U.S.A.

#451. "A soldier's life is a succession of extremes, first a long period of inactivity, followed by a [a period] when all his energies both mental and physical are taxed to the utmost."
* A Yankee soldier named James T. Miller. May 1863.

#452. "These are the first "Cartridges" that I have ever seen, and is it possible that we are actually to kill men? Human beings? ...Yes, this is war and how hardened men must become."
* The thoughts of Confederate soldier Edmund DeWitt upon receiving his first supply of ammunition.

#453. "A man ceases to be himself when he enlists in the ranks."
* Confederate Lieutenant Leonidas Polk, spring 1863. Polk was a North Carolinian, an Episcopal bishop, and then he became a general. He was killed by a Parrott rifle on June 14, 1864, at Pine Mountain, Georgia. Parrot rifles were muzzle-loading rifled artillery.

#454. "Death is a common lot of all and the diferance between dyeing to day and to morrow is not much but we all prefer to morrow."
* A Union soldier from Maine named M. P. Larry.

#455. "The rule in North Carolina seems to be that it takes two houses to make a town & that three and a barn make a city."
* A Union soldier named Samuel Storrow. November 1862.

#456. "This place would be quite pleasant if it had been all burned up."
* A Union soldier from Connecticut named John Crosby voicing his opinion of swampy Donaldsonville, Louisiana. July 1863.

#457. "The country about here reminds me more of New England than any place I have seen and the climate reminds me more of that infernal place down below that I have not seen but often heard of."
* Union Sergeant Henry C. Hall was from New England, where the climate is cooler than that of the South. In August 1862 Hall found himself in

Fredericksburg, Virginia during a typically hot southern August.

#458. "This country is so beautiful I wish I had been born there."
* Corporal Edward Whitaker regarding the countryside of Alexandria in northern Virginia, June 1861. Whitaker was from Connecticut.

#459. "Sand flies, midges, mosquitoes, stinging ants, little red ticks...leave very little of us."
* Some hardships of war as described by Union Lieutenant John Appleton writing to his wife. Appleton was in South Carolina as a member of the 54th Massachusetts Volunteer Infantry Regiment led by Colonel Robert Gould Shaw. This regiment was made up of African-American soldiers who would fight bravely at Fort Wagner in June 1863. The 54th Massachusetts suffered great casualties at Fort Wagner.

#460.
"Mary Jackson is my name
Single is my station
Happy will be the soldier boy—
Who makes the alteration."
* In June of 1862, the Sanitary Commission in Bowling Green, Kentucky found this note pinned to a quilt that was to be distributed to Union troops. Apparently, the single Mary Jackson used notes on quilts to help her find a husband. Clever girl! Let's hope Mary found her guy.

#461. "We cook and eat, talk and laugh with the enemy's dead lying all about us as though they were so many hogs."
* Confederate Captain Samuel T. Foster.

#462. "In camp. I must say that I feel down in the mouth, only paid a week ago and have not a cent now, having bluffed away all that I did not send home. I don't think I will play poker any more."
* Jacob E. Hyneman writing in his diary on February 20, 1864. Hyneman was a soldier in Grant's army.

#463.
"Description of the Confederate Soldier
Pvt. Carlton McCarthy
Richmond Howitzers

"Reduced to the minimum, the private soldier consisted of one man, one hat, one jacket, one shirt, one pair of pants, one pair of drawers, one pair of shoes, and one pair of socks. His baggage was one blanket, one rubber blanket, and one haversack. The haversack contained smoking tobacco and a pipe and generally a small piece of soap, with temporary additions of apples, persimmons, blackberries, and such other commodities as he could pick up on the march.

"Common white cotton shirts and drawers proved the best...(for) the common private. The infantry ...carried their caps and cartridges in their pockets. Canteens...were discarded. A good strong tin cup was better... easier to fill at a well...and serviceable as a boiler for making coffee.

"(Each soldiers) one blanket and one rubber cloth were rolled lengthwise, with the rubber cloth outside, tying the ends together and throwing the loop over the left shoulder... the (tied) ends hanging under the right arm."
* A Confederate soldier's articles, 1865. Note the listing of a rubber blanket. During the Civil War waterproof blankets and garments were available. General Thomas Jonathan "Stonewall" Jackson was wounded by friendly fire while wearing a waterproof coat. Jackson's coat, with a bullet hole plainly visible in the back of the upper left arm, is on display at the Virginia Military Institute (VMI) in Lexington, Virginia.

#464. "Our men are not good soldiers. They brag, but don't perform, complain sadly if they don't get everything they want, and a march of a few miles uses them up. It will take a long time to overcome these things, and what is in store for us in the future I know not."
* General William Tecumseh Sherman, 1861. These comments were made by Sherman early in the Civil War after the first Battle of Bull Run. The shortcomings of the Union soldiers would change for the better as the war progressed. Men had to learn and train to become soldiers.

#465. "The officers have all the glory. Glory is not for the private soldier, such as die in the hospitals, being eat up with the deadly gangrene, and being imperfectly waited on. Glory is for generals, colonels, majors, captains, and lieutenants. They have all the glory, and when the poor private wins battles by dint of sweat, hard marches, camp and picket duty, fasting and broken bones, the officers get all the glory."
* Confederate Sam Watkins.

#466. "I was severe, but endeavored to be just, for I knew if we could not command our men, we had no business to attempt invasion."
* General William Tecumseh Sherman.

#467. "You can't bring tents; tent flies without poles, if you must, or tents cut down to that size, and only as few as are indispensable. No mess-chests or trunks. It is better to leave these things where you are than to throw them away after starting. The road to glory cannot be followed with much baggage."
* Confederate General Richard Ewell regarding how everything brought on a march must be carried somehow, either by horse, by horse and wagon, or by manpower. Excess weight and baggage would soon be tossed away because it was simply not worth the effort to carry it.

#468. "We enlisted to put down the rebellion, and had no patience with the red-tape tom-foolery of the regular service. Furthermore, our boys recognized no superiors except in the line of legitimate duty. Shoulder straps waived, a private was ready at the drop of a hat to thrash his commander; a feat that occurred more than once."
* An unknown Union private from Indiana early in the Civil War.

#469. "We will fight you to the death. Better to die a thousand deaths than to submit and live under you and your Negro allies."
* Confederate General John Bell Hood.

#470. "Colonel, I yield to no man in sympathy, but I am obliged to sweat these men tonight so I may save their blood tomorrow."

* General Thomas Jonathan "Stonewall" Jackson's reply to a fellow officer who was urging Jackson to give his men a rest during a march in the Valley Campaign.

#471. "The time for war has not yet come, but it will come, and that soon. And when it does come, my advice is to draw the sword and throw away the scabbard."
* Professor Thomas Jonathan Jackson's advice to cadets at the Virginia Military Institute (VMI) on April 13, 1861. On April 12, 1861, the Civil War began with the bombardment of Fort Sumter. Jackson and the troops he led in the Civil War drew their swords, and they were very successful fighting the Yankees.

#472. "Good soldiers are never flogged, and there is no more hardship or disgrace to them in bad ones being punished than there is to good people in murderers being hanged."
* Captain Fitzgerald Ross, 1865. Ross was an Austrian and an observer with General Robert E. Lee's Army of Northern Virginia during the Gettysburg campaign.

#473. "What's the use of killing Yankees? You kill one and six appear in his place."
* The thoughts of a discouraged Confederate soldier after Gettysburg.

#474. "You for one have met your just reward, which is a grant of land from the Confederates of three feet by six, in an obscure spot, where your friends if you have any, will never be able to find your body, for there is nothing to mark the spot except a small hillock of red clay, which a few hard rains will wash away."
* A Confederate named J. C. Salter spoke these words at the grave of a Union soldier on July 11, 1864.

#475. "They talk about the ravages of the enemy in their marches through the country, but I do not think that the Yankees are any worse than our own army."

* Robert Patrick of the 4th Louisiana writing on May 21, 1864, as he observed dairy and poultry products being taken from a Southern lady by Confederate soldiers. The Confederate States of America made an act of impressment on March 26, 1863, that allowed the army to take from citizens supplies necessary for the war effort.

#476. "[As a soldier in the Union Army I belong to] Uncle Sam, mentally, morally, and physically. Therefore, My virtues and vices must correspond to that of my fellows; I must lie to rebels, steal from rebels and kill rebels;-- Uncle Sam making vicarious atonement for these sins."
* A Union soldier named John F. Holahan explaining in 1862 on how he figured the government was to take the responsibility and the blame for his wartime sins.

#477. "The rebels cannot increase their forces in the field. They already have out every available man, and great numbers of conscripts are worthless as soldiers from physical infirmities. I have seen men with hollow chests...and some even with but one Arm, men with an eye gone and a great many worthless from general debility-and feeble constitutions, fit only for Hospitals."
* This is from an 1863 letter to Abraham Lincoln written by General Neal Dow. Dow was a prisoner of war at Libby prison in Richmond, Virginia. He was a Quaker, but Dow was dismissed from the Society of Friends because of his war activities.

#478.
"Who are you?"
"We are two men of the Twelfth Georgia, carrying a wounded comrade to the hospital."
"Don't you know you are in the Union lines?"
"No."
"You are. Go to your right."
"Man, you've got a heart in you."
 * A Union sentry gives friendly directions to some lost Confederate soldiers at the Second Battle of Bull Run. August 1862.

#479. "Hant you got no better clothes than those?"
"You are a set of damned fools-do you suppose we put on our good clothes to go out and kill damned dogs?"
* A conversation between a Billy Yank and a Johnny Reb during the siege of Atlanta, Georgia in November 1862.

#480. "They are sick and tired and if we will stack arms and go home they will do the same and hang their Ringleaders."
* A Union soldier tells what he learned from a Confederate in December 1862.

#481. "Knives spoons pipes money and most anything."
* A Union soldier near Falmouth, Virginia in December 1862, when Union and Confederate troops met in an informal truce to trade items. Informal truces of front-line troops were not unusual. A temporary friendly agreement of something like, "I won't shoot you if you won't shoot me..." could be established between the Billy Yanks and Johnny Rebs.

#482.
"Gents U.S. Army

We send you some Tobacco by our Packet. Send us some coffee in return. Also a deck of cards if you have them, and we will send you more tobacco. Send us any late papers if you have them.

Jas. O. Parker
Co. H. 17th Regt. Miss. Vols."
* This was attached to a "miniature boat six inches long" and floated down the Rappahannock River toward Union troops from New Jersey. The Rebels would trade whiskey and tobacco for coffee and newspapers from the Yankees.

#483.
"Reb: When is Grant going to march into Vicksburg?"
"Yank: When you get your last mule and dog eat up."
* At Vicksburg, Mississippi M. Ebeneezer Wescott recorded this hollered

discussion between a Billy Yank and a Johnny Reb in early July 1863. Vicksburg would soon fall to the Yankees on July 4, 1863. The Confederates were defeated at Gettysburg, Pennsylvania the day before.

#484. "The rebels had their lines already made. Under cover of the night our lines were pushed close to theirs. We made a bargain with them that we would not fire on them if they would not fire on us, and they were as good as their word. It seems too bad that we have to fight men that we like. Now these southern soldiers seem just like our own boys, only they are on the other side. They talk about their people at home, their mothers and fathers and their sweethearts just as we do among ourselves. Both sides did a lot of talking back and forth, but there was no shooting until I came off duty in the morning."

"June 25th. When the pickets came off the line this morning they had quite a pretty story to tell of how they chummed it with some Louisiana rebs. A company of our Indiana boys met a company of Louisiana rebels half way between the two lines. They stacked arms, shook hands, exchanged papers, swapped tobacco, told each other a lot of things about their feelings and how they wished the war would end so they might go back to their homes and be good friends again, shook hands once more with tears in their eyes as they bid goodbye forever, and after calling to each other to be sure that both sides were ready, commenced a furious fire on each other."
* Chauncey H. Cooke was a volunteer Union soldier from Wisconsin who was camped near Kennesaw Mountain, Georgia on June 24, 1864. These are two excerpts from a letter he wrote to his parents.

#485. "The fire opened—bang, bang, bang, a rattle de bang, bang, bang, a boom, de bang, bang, bang, boom, bang, boom, bang, boom, bang, boom, whirr-siz-siz-siz--a ripping, roaring, boom, bang!"
* Confederate Sam Watkins describing a "fire fight." Sam Watkins was twenty-one-years-old and from Columbia, Tennessee when he joined up to fight in the Civil War. He kept a journal and recorded his experiences and thoughts during the war. His words give us great insight into the Civil War.

#486. "Eyes right, guide center. Close-up, guide right, halt, forward, right oblique, left oblique, halt, forward, guide center, eyes right, dress up

promptly in the rear, steady, double quick, charge bayonets, fire at will."
* Confederate Sam Watkins describing the orders his regiment received at Shiloh.

#487. "You have heard frequently of the wild excitement of battle. I experience no such feelings. There is a sense of depression continually working away at my heart, caused by a knowledge of the great suffering in store for large numbers of my fellow men."
* The words of Confederate soldier William Nugent.

#488. "There was men laying wanting help, wanting water, with blood running out them and the top or sides their heads gone, great big holes in them. I just promises the good Lord if He just let me git out of that mess, I wouldn't run off no more, but I didn't know then He wasn't gwine let me pout with just that battle."
* The after-battle observations and thoughts of an ex-slave named Thomas Cole.

#489. "We heard all through the war that the army 'was eager to be led against the enemy.' It must have been so, for truthful correspondents said so, and editors confirmed it; but when you came to hunt for this particular itch it was always the next regiment that had it. The truth is, when bullets are whacking against tree trunks and solid shot are cracking skulls like eggshells, the consuming passion in the breast of the average man is to get out of the way. Between the physical fear of going forward, and the moral fear of turning back, there is a predicament of exceptional awkwardness, from which a hidden hole in the ground would be a wonderfully welcome outlet."
* David Thompson, a Union private from New York.

#490. "I have bin in one battle and that satisfied me with war and I would beg to be excused next time. for I tell you that there cannons and the shot and shell flying as thick as hail and the grape and cannister flying between the shot and shells."
* Confederate soldier Haburn R. Foster tells of the fright and horror of a battlefield. July 1862.

#491. "If men were not afraid to die it would simplify matters very much. They are afraid & fear makes them run."
* Union General Oliver Otis Howard after the Battle of Chancellorsville. Howard was a prominent general, he lost his right arm and suffered another serious wound at The Battle of Seven Pines/Fair Oaks fought on May 31 and June 1, 1862. Later in 1893, he was awarded the Medal of Honor for his service at The Battle of Seven Pines/Fair Oaks. He founded and was president of Howard University. Howard wrote much on military and historical subjects, but never anything regarding the Civil War.

#492. "In many instances arms and legs and sometimes heads protrude and my attention has been directed to several places where hogs were actually rooting out the bodies and devouring them."
* A gruesome description of the Gettysburg battlefield three weeks after the battle was fought. This quote is from a letter written to Pennsylvania's Governor Andrew Curtin by David Wills. Wills was a Gettysburg banker and civic leader.

#493. "Sometimes it looked like the war was about to cut my ears off. I would lay stretched out on the ground and bullets would fly over my head. I would take a rock and place it on top of my head, thinking it would keep the bullets from going through my brain."
* From an African-American soldier.

#494. "Unnamed, unknown, remain, and still remain, the bravest soldiers. Our manliest--our boys--our hardy darlings: no picture gives them. Likely, the typical one of them (standing, no doubt, for hundreds, thousands) crawls aside to some bush-clump, or ferny tuft, on receiving his death-shot--there, sheltering a little while, soaking roots, grass and soil, with red blood--the battle advances, retreats, flits from the scene, sweeps by--and there, haply with pain and suffering (yet less, far less, than is supposed,) the last lethargy winds like a serpent round him--the eyes glaze in death—none recks—perhaps the burial-squads, in truce, a week afterwards, search not the secluded spot—and there, at last, the Bravest Soldier, crumbles in mother earth, unburied and unknown."

* Poet Walt Whitman, 1865.

#495. "We live so mean here and the hard bread is all worms and the meat stinks like hell...and rice to or three times a week & worms as long as your finger. I liked rice once but god damn the stuff now."
* A Yankee soldier named H. Holden expressing his displeasure with military food in August 1862.

#496. "I fear this liquor more than Pope's army."
* Confederate General Thomas Jonathan "Stonewall" Jackson. Stonewall was a pious man who did not drink alcohol. He was giving instructions at Manassas, Virginia, in August 1862 to a captain about dumping barrels of whiskey found in a warehouse. Stonewall wanted to prevent his men from overindulging in the "Oh! Be Joyful."

#497.
"Whiskey is a monster, and ruins great and small,
But in our noble army, Headquarters gets it all;
They drink it when there's danger, although it seems too hard,
But if a private touches it they put him 'under guard.'"
* A verse from a Southern soldiers' song named "The Brass-Mounted Army."

#498. "We live on crackers so hard that if we loaded our guns with them we could of killed seceshs in a hurry."
* The comments of a Union private from Illinois. The crackers referred to in this quote are most likely what was known as hardtack. Hardtack was a cracker made from a recipe of flour, shortening, salt, and water. Hardtack and black coffee were common staples of the soldiers.

#499. "If I ever lose my patriotism, and the "secesh" spirit dies out, then you may know the "Commissary" is at fault. Corn meal mixed with water and tough beef three times a day will knock the "Brave Volunteer" under quicker than Yankee bullets."
* A Confederate soldier named Robert P. Banks, October 1862. Salt beef

(also called salt horse) was a common food eaten during the Civil War. Salt beef was pickled beef that was preserved by soaking it in a very strong brine. The pickling often resulted in such salty meat that it would have to be soaked in water before it could be eaten. The pickling often failed and the meat became rancid.

#500.
"Our generals eat the poultry, and buy it very cheap,
Our Colonels and our Majors devour hog and sheep;
The Privates are contented (except when they can steal),
With beef and corn bread plenty to make a hearty meal."
* A verse from Southern soldiers' song named "The Brass-Mounted Army."

#501. "We are in Loudon county, one of the richest in the state. The people hereabouts are said to be leaning towards the Union, and so we deal as gently with them as we can. There are plenty of nice fence rails. Of course we must have our coffee and a fire to cook it; so I hope the good people of Loudon county can spare a few rails from their fences. There are some nice turkeys too, and a gobbler is gobbled up and brought to camp, where he is very much welcomed. Now the good people will remember us, for we spared them the trouble, in a good many instances, of feeding the corn to their turkeys and chickens, which they may need before this cruel war is over."
* A Union soldier in Virginia explaining tongue-in-cheek why it was appropriate for the Yankee soldiers to eat Confederate turkeys. Note the correct spelling of the Virginia county is "Loudoun." Soldiers would often spell words as they sounded

A BONUS Quote and Note! :-)

#502."I make up my opinions from facts and reasoning, and not to suit anybody but myself. If people don't like my opinions, it makes little difference as I don't solicit their opinions or votes."
* General William Tecumseh Sherman.

A Johnny Reb:
William H. Rockwell, Pvt., North Carolina,
18th Infantry, Company H

Thank You For Reading

This book was meant to help you learn about Civil War history from the words of those who lived it and made it.

I have been learning about the Civil War ever since my family took a trip to Gettysburg when I was seven-years-old. The entire three-day Battle of Gettysburg was more than I could absorb and comprehend at that young age, but by the end of the visit I had acquired, as best a seven-year-old could, a basic understanding of what happened at Gettysburg. At the Gettysburg Museum and Visitor Center, my father bought me a Gettysburg young reader's book by MacKinlay Kantor. That book began for me a life-long quest or hobby of learning about the Civil War. I still have that Kantor Civil War book. It's part of my Civil War library and I've read it as an adult. I'm still learning about Gettysburg today.

The Civil War is an inexhaustible subject. There is much to learn. Although there are and have been, many esteemed historians and authors of the Civil War such as Bruce Catton, Shelby Foote, James McPherson, Stephen Sears, Jeff Shaara, Michael Shaara, Gary Gallagher, Brian Pohanka, Eric Foner, David Blight, Allen C. Guelzo, and... well, this list could go on and on, but those are some I hold in high regard. Despite their great expertise, I suppose none of these historians and authors knew or know everything there is to learn about the Civil War.

In addition to learning about the overall scope of Civil War history, I have also enjoyed picking up interesting bits of information about the Civil War. There's always some quote, fact, or note about some leader, battle, place, or person of the Civil War which I find interesting or curious. So, I make note of it by either underlining the text in the book I'm reading or by jotting it down in a notebook.

A few examples of Civil War facts or notes I've collected:

* Abolitionist John Brown was at the Hudson, Ohio Congregational Church in 1837 attending a fervent prayer meeting held to honor Elijah P. Lovejoy. Lovejoy was an abolitionist and newspaperman who had been killed by a

pro-slavery mob in Alton, Illinois. Brown sat in the back of the church listening quietly during the prayer meeting. As the meeting was coming to an end, John Brown stood and raised his right hand and made his public vow, "Here, before God, in the presence of these witnesses, from this time, I consecrate my life to the destruction of slavery."

* The Union used two-wheeled ambulances to remove wounded from the battlefield. These two-wheeled conveyances were unsteady, they sometimes tipped over and spilled the wounded out onto the ground. The soldiers gave such an ambulance the name, "Avalanche."

* The Swamp Angel was a 16,700 pound Parrot rifle located at a Union battery 4 1/2 miles from Confederate-held Charleston, South Carolina. The Swamp Angel had an 8-inch-diameter bore, an 11-foot bore depth, and a 17-pound powder charge. The Swamp Angel was a huge gun. This giant cannon could fire a 200 pound projectile into the heart of Charleston. The Swamp Angel's purpose was to bring Charleston to its knees so the Yankees could gain control of the city. On August 22-23, 1863, the Swamp Angel went to work on Charleston, sending its massive projectiles into the city. But, on one firing, its final shot, the Swamp Angel exploded, its breech blown out by the cannon's own power. The damage to Charleston by the Swamp Angel was minimal and the Confederates kept control of the city. The Swamp Angel was eventually sold as scrap iron and it was purchased by the city of Trenton, New Jersey. Trenton chose not to destroy the Swamp Angel. If you would like to see it, the Swamp Angel is mounted at a park in Trenton.

* President Rutherford B. Hayes fought in the Civil War with the Twenty-Third Ohio. Hayes became a brevet major general and later in life he referred to his Civil War years as "the best years" of his life.

* Ulysses S. Grant took Vicksburg, Mississippi on July 4, 1863. It has incorrectly been said that Vicksburg did not "officially" celebrate the Fourth of July again until 1945. It is a myth that Vicksburg never celebrated the Fourth of July from 1863 to 1945. Feelings were strong and there was bitterness after July 4, 1863, and so for some the Fourth was not an occasion for celebration. Others did celebrate. Some informal Fourth of July celebrations, a large one in 1907 and smaller ones afterward, did take place in Vicksburg between 1863 and 1945. In 1945, with World War II coming to an end (Officially on September 2, 1945.) and with the Allies

victorious, Vicksburg had a rebirth of patriotism and the Fourth of July was a reason to celebrate.

* When Robert E. Lee surrendered to Ulysses S. Grant at Appomattox Court House on April 9, 1865, Lee wore a new full-dress uniform that included a sash and a sword studded with jewels. Grant's uniform was plain at the surrender. Nothing flashy for Grant.

This is the first of four books I have planned that will be about Civil War quotes, notes, or facts. In this book, I shared with you some of the interesting Civil War quotes and notes I've collected over time, but I have more.

I hope I have helped you to learn some things about the Civil War. Thank you for reading *501 Civil War Quotes and Notes*.

Jonathan R. Allen
Pinehurst, North Carolina
March, 2018
LearnCivilWarHistory@gmail.com

Learn more about the Civil War at my website:
LearnCivilWarHistory.com

Follow me on Twitter and learn Civil War history from my Tweets:
@CivilWarHistory

Bibliography

Below is the list of resources used for the quotes and notes included in this book. This list is a good place to start for anyone who wants to read and learn more about the Civil War.

Books

The Civil War: A Narrative, by Shelby Foote
Vol I: *Fort Sumter to Perryville*
Vol II: *Fredericksburg to Meridian*
Vol III: *Red River to Appomattox*

Stars in Their Courses: The Gettysburg Campaign June-July 1863, by Shelby Foote

The Centennial History of the Civil War, by Bruce Catton
Vol I: *The Coming Fury*
Vol II: *Terrible Swift Sword*
Vol III: *Never Call Retreat*

The Army of the Potomac, by Bruce Catton
Vol I: *Mr. Lincoln's Army*
Vol II: *Glory Road*
Vol III: A Stillness at Appomattox

The Civil War, by Bruce Catton

Grant Moves South, by Bruce Catton

Grant Takes Command, by Bruce Catton

The American Heritage Picture History of The Civil War, by Bruce Catton

Battle Cry of Freedom, by James M. McPherson

The Civil War Dictionary, by Mark M. Boatner III

The Library of Congress Civil War Desk Reference

The Civil War (PBS series and book), by Ward/Burns/Burns

Lincoln at Gettysburg, by Garry Willis

The Civil War Day by Day, by E.B. Long with Barbara Long

Gettysburg, by MacKinlay Cantor

The Illustrated Directory of Uniforms, Weapons, and Equipment of the Civil War, by David Miller, editor

National Geographic Guide to the Civil War National Battlefield Parks, by Greene/Gallagher

The Day Dixie Died, by Thomas and Debra Goodrich

Everyday Life in the 1800s, by Marc McCutcheon

The Lincoln Nobody Knows, by Webb Garrison

The Civil War Years, by Robert E. Denney

Traveling the Underground Railroad, by Bruce Chadwick

Dancing Along the Deadline, by Ezra Hoyt Ripple, edited by Mark A. Snell

Don't Know Much About The Civil War, by Kenneth C. Davis

Mathew Brady: Historian With a Camera, by James D. Horan

The Commanders of the Civil War, by William C. Davis

The Battlefields of the Civil War, by William C. Davis

The Great Invasion, by Jacob Hoke

They Met at Gettysburg, by General Edward J. Stackpole

Captain Robert E. Lee, Recollections and Letters of General Robert E. Lee by Captain Robert E. Lee, His Son, by Captain Robert E. Lee

Marching Through Georgia, by Lee Kennett

A Diary From Dixie, by Mary Chesnut

Sherman, by B.H. Liddell Hart

Sherman's March, by Burke Davis

Lincoln, by David Herbert Donald

Four years campaigning in the army of the Potomac, by Daniel G. Crotty

None Died in Vain: The Saga of the American Civil War, by Robert Leckie

Stonewall: A Biography of General Thomas J. Jackson, by Byron Farwell

Prose Works 1892: Speciman Days, by Walt Whitman, Floyd Stovall

Afro-American history: past to present, by Henry N. Drewry, Cecilia H. Drewry

The Science of War - A Collection of Essays and Lectures 1891-1903, by G. R. Henderson

Co. Aytch, by Samuel R. Watkins

A Badger Boy in Blue: The Civil War Letters of Chauncey H. Cooke, by Chauncey Herbert Cooke, William H. Mulligan

The Life of Billy Yank: The Common Soldier of the Union, by Bell Irvin Wile

City Under Siege: Richmond in the Civil War, by Mike Wright

Living Hell: The Dark Side of the Civil War, by Michael C. C. Adams

Reluctant Rebel: The Secret Diary of Robert Patrick, 1861-1865, by Robert Patrick, Foster Jay Taylor

The Civil War Soldier: Ideology and Experience, by Reid Hardeman Mitchell

Cities and Camps of the Confederate States, FitzGerald Ross, by Richard Barksdale Harwell

Rebel Yell: The Violence, Passion, and Redemption of Stonewall Jackson, by S. C. Gwynne

I Am Me, by Ten Speed Press Staff

Voices from the Civil War Reader's Theater Script, by Timothy Rasinski, Lorraine Griffith

This Hallowed Ground: A History of the Civil War, by Bruce Catton

They Called Him Stonewall: A Life of Lieutenant General T. J. Jackson, CSA, by Burke Davis

Home Letters of General Sherman, by William Tecumseh Sherman

No Soap, No Pay, Diarrhea, Dysentery & Desertion: A Composite Diary of the ..., by Jeff Toalson

The Civil War Soldier: A Historical Reader, by Michael Barton, Larry M. Logue

Blue-Eyed Child of Fortune: The Civil War Letters of Colonel Robert Gould Shaw, by Robert Gould Shaw

Through the Canebrake, by William McCollough

The Life of Billy Yank: The Common Soldier of the Union, by Bell Irvin Wiley, James I. Robertson, Jr.

New Perspectives on Race and Slavery in America: Essays in Honor of

501 Civil War Quotes and Notes

Kenneth ..., by Robert H. Abzug, Stephen E. Maizlish

The Civil War Soldier: A Historical Reader, by Michael Barton, Larry M. Logue

The Seven-Day Scholar: The Civil War: Exploring History One Week at a Time, by Dennis Gaffney, Peter Gaffney

Unto a Good Land: A History of the American People, Volume 1: To 1900, by David Edwin Harrell, Jr., Edwin S. Gaustad, John B. Boles

God's Almost Chosen Peoples: A Religious History of the American Civil War, by George C. Rable

The Enduring Relevance of Robert E. Lee: The Ideological Warfare..., by Marshall L. DeRosa

Both Prayed to the Same God: Religion and Faith in the American Civil War, by Robert J. Miller

Lee the American, by Gamaliel Bradford

Massachusetts Quilts: Our Common Wealth, by Lynne Z. Bassett

God's Almost Chosen Peoples: A Religious History of the American Civil War, by George C. Rable

Now the Drum of War: Walt Whitman and His Brothers in the Civil War, by Robert Roper

Lee In the Shadow of Washington, by Richard B. McCaslin

America Out Loud: The Most Inspirational, Irreverent, Intelligent, Ignorant ..., by Alan Axelrod

The American Spirit: United States History as Seen by Contemporaries, Volume 1, by David Kennedy, Thomas Bailey

The Civil War: The Final Year Told by Those Who Lived It: (Library of ..., by Aaron Sheehan-Dean

A History of American Civil War Literature, by Coleman Hutchison

Union--disunion--reunion, by Samuel Sullivan Cox

Of the People, by the People, for the People: And Other Quotations, by Abraham Lincoln, G. S. Boritt

Life and Letters of Robert Edward Lee, by J.W. Jones

The Eloquent President: A Portrait of Lincoln Through His Words, by Ronald C. White

Hitch Your Wagon to a Star and Other Quotations from Ralph Waldo Emerson, by Keith Frome, Ralph Waldo Emerson

Freedom on My Mind: The Columbia Documentary History of the African American ..., by Manning Marable, John McMillian, Nishani Frazier

A Buff Looks at the American Civil War: A Look at the United States ..., by Shon Powers

History of the Southern Confederacy, by Clement Eaton

Jefferson Davis, American, by William J. Cooper

Ballads & Songs of the Civil War for Guitar, by Jerry Silverman

Black Reconstruction in America 1860-1880, by W. E. B. Du Bois, David Levering Lewis

Josie Underwood's Civil War Diary, by Josie Underwood

The Rebellion Record: A Diary of American Events, with Documents ..., Volume 7, by Frank Moore

Strange True Stories of Louisiana, by George Washington Cable

Government of Our Own: The Making of the Confederacy, by William C. Davis

Tried by War: Abraham Lincoln as Commander in Chief, by James M. McPherson

Abraham Lincoln: The Prairie Years and the War Years, by Carl Sandburg

The American Past: A Survey of American History, Enhanced Edition, by Joseph Conlin

Reminiscences of the Civil War, by John Brown Gordon

Trials and Triumphs: The Women of the American Civil War, by Marilyn Mayer Culpepper

The Confederate Reader: How the South Saw the War, by Richard B. Harwell

Yankee Blitzkrieg: Wilson's Raid through Alabama and Georgia, by James Pickett Jones

This Mighty Scourge: Perspectives on the Civil War, by James M. McPherson

Sherman: A Soldier's Passion for Order, by John F. Marszalek

Confederate Military History: A Library of Confederate States History, Volume 3, by Clement Anselm Evans

The Complete Papers And Writings Of Abraham Lincoln (Biographically ..., by Abraham Lincoln

Ploughshares Into Swords: Josiah Gorgas and Confederate Ordnance, by Frank Everson Vandiver

Lincoln Addresses and Letters, by Abraham Lincoln

And Keep Moving On: The Virginia Campaign, May-June 1864, by Mark Grimsley

The Vicksburg Campaign, March 29-May 18, 1863, by Steven E.

Woodworth, Charles D Grear

Stonewall Jackson, by Hunter McGuire, United Confederate Veterans. R.E. Lee Camp, No. 1

The Selected Papers of Thaddeus Stevens, Volume 1: April 1865-August 1868, by Thaddeus Stevens

The Fort Pillow Massacre: North, South, and the Status of African Americans ..., by Bruce Tap

The River Was Dyed with Blood: Nathan Bedford Forrest and Fort Pillow, by Brian Steel Wills

Union & Emancipation: Essays on Politics and Race in the Civil War Era, by David W. Blight, Brooks D. Simpson

Lincoln's Notebooks: Letters, Speeches, Journals, and Poems, by Dan Tucker

A History of the Negro Troops in the War of Rebellion, 1861-1865, by George Washington Williams

A Pocket History of the Civil War: Citizen Soldiers, Bloody Battles, and the ..., by Martin Graham

United States Congressional Serial Set, Volume 2762

Ken Burns's The Civil War Deluxe eBook (Enhanced Edition): An Illustrated ..., by Geoffrey C. Ward, Ric Burns, Ken Burns

Black Troops, White Commanders and Freedmen During the Civil War, by Howard Westwood

The Negro's Civil War: How American Blacks Felt and Acted During the War for ..., by James M. McPherson

A People's History of the Civil War: Struggles for the Meaning of Freedom, by David Williams

War, Terrible War, by Joy Hakim

Abraham Lincoln and the Road to Emancipation, 1861-1865, by William K. Klingaman

Sherman's Civil War: Selected Correspondence of William T. Sherman, 1860-1865, by Brooks D. Simpson, Jean V. Berlin

After the Civil War: The Heroes, Villains, Soldiers, and Civilians Who ..., by James Robertson

Impeached: The Trial of President Andrew Johnson and the Fight for Lincoln's ..., by David O. Stewart

Bold Dragoon: The Life of J.E.B. Stuart, by Emory M. Thomas

War News: Gray in Black & White: Newspapers in the Civil War, by Brayton Harris

New Orleans: A Pictorial History, by Leonard Victor Huber

As If It Were Glory: Robert Beecham's Civil War from the Iron Brigade to the ..., by Michael E. Stevens

Partisan Life with Mosby's Rangers (Abridged, Annotated), by Major John Scott

The Mosby Myth: A Confederate Hero in Life and Legend, by Paul Ashdown, Edward Caudill

Documentary History of Reconstruction: Political, Military, Social ..., Volume 1, by Walter Lynwood Fleming

The Destructive War: William Tecumseh Sherman, Stonewall Jackson, and the ..., by Charles Royster

The Oxford Book of the American South: Testimony, Memory, and Fiction, by Edward L. Ayers, Bradley C. Mittendorf

Look Away!: A History of the Confederate States of America, by William

C. Davis

Mothers of Invention: Women of the Slaveholding South in the American Civil War, by Drew Gilpin Faust

The Civil War in America, by Sir William Howard Russell

The Road to Appomattox Bell, by Irvin Wiley

History of Kentucky, by Lewis Collins, Richard H. Collins

Journal of American Folklore, Volume 5

Browser's Book of Texas Quotations, by Steven A. Jent

General Lee's Army: From Victory to Collapse, by Joseph Glatthaar

The Confederacy, by Charles P. Roland

Songs of the Civil War, by Irwin Silber, Jerry Silverman

The Conservative Review, Volume 4, by Walter Neale

Mary Chesnut's Civil War, by Mary Boykin Miller Chesnut, Comer Vann Woodward

Why the Civil War Came, by Gabor S. Boritt

Confederate Rage, Yankee Wrath: No Quarter in the Civil War, by George S Burkhardt

Civil War America: Voices from the Home Front, by James Alan Marten

United States Congressional serial set, Issue 3112

Secession as an International Phenomenon: From America's Civil War to ..., by Don H. Doyle

Why the Confederacy Lost, by Gabor S. Boritt

Rhett: The Turbulent Life and Times of a Fire-eater, by William C. Davis

Shifting Grounds: Nationalism and the American South, 1848-1865, by Paul Quigley

Lincoln on Democracy, by Abraham Lincoln, G. S. Boritt

Black Confederates and Afro-Yankees in Civil War Virginia, by Ervin L. Jordan

A Visitation of God: Northern Civilians Interpret the Civil War, by Sean A. Scott

In the Hands of Providence: Joshua L. Chamberlain and the American Civil War, by Alice Rains Trulock

American History through its Greatest Speeches: A Documentary History of the ..., by Jolyon P. Girard, Darryl Mace, Courtney Smith

The Lincoln Nobody Knows, by Richard N. Current

Lincoln's Greatest Speech: The Second Inaugural, by Ronald C. White

The Lincoln-Douglas Debates of 1858, Volume 3, by Abraham Lincoln, Stephen Arnold Douglas

Lincoln's Story: The Wayfarer, by Vel

Generals in Blue and Gray: Lincoln's Generals, by Wilmer L. Jones

Reluctant Rebels: The Confederates Who Joined the Army after 1861, by Kenneth W. Noe

Home Letters of General Sherman, by William Tecumseh Sherman

The Poems of Herman Melville, by Herman Melville, Douglas Robillard

The Life of Johnny Reb: The Common Soldier of the Confederacy, by Bell Irvin Wiley

Fields of Fury, by James M. McPherson

Robert E. Lee and the Southern Confederacy, 1807-1870, by Henry Alexander White

The Lincoln Assassination, by John Butler Ford

Nashville: The Western Confederacy's Final Gamble, by James L. McDonough

Shrouds of Glory: From Atlanta to Nashville: The Last Great Campaign of the ..., by Winston Groom

Master of War: The Life of General George H. Thomas, by Benson Bobrick

Robert E. Lee, Man and Soldier, Volume 2, by Thomas Nelson Page

Lee's Lieutenants Third Volume Abridged: A Study in Command, by Douglas Southall Freeman

Lee: The Last Years, by Charles Bracelen Flood

The Army of Northern Virginia in 1862, by William Allan

Ulysses S. Grant: Triumph Over Adversity, 1822-1865, by Brooks Simpson

LINCOLN & DAVIS: A Dual Biography of America's Civil War Presidents, by Augustin Stucker

Fighting Men of the Civil War, by William C. Davis, Russ A. Pritchard

Robert E. Lee and the Fall of the Confederacy, 1863-1865, by Ethan Sepp Rafuse

The Gleam of Bayonets: The Battle of Antietam and Robert E. Lee's Maryland ..., by James V. Murfin, James I. Robertson, Scott Hartwig

History of the Colored Race in America, by William T. Alexander

General James Longstreet: The Confederacy's Most Controversial Soldier, by Jeffry D. Wert

Memoirs and Selected Letters: Personal Memoirs of U.S. Grant, Selected ..., by Ulysses Simpson Grant

Vicksburg, 1863, by Winston Groom

Battles and Leaders of the Civil War, Volume 3, by Robert Underwood Johnson, Clarence Clough Buel

Every Day of the Civil War: A Chronological Encyclopedia, by Bud Hannings

House of Abraham: Lincoln and the Todds, a Family Divided by War, by Stephen Berry

Major Robert Anderson and Fort Sumter, 1861, by Eliza McIntosh Clinch Anderson Lawton

America's God and Country: Encyclopedia of Quotations, by William Joseph Federer

A General Who Will Fight: The Leadership of Ulysses S. Grant, by Harry S. Laver

Magazines:

America's Civil War

Civil War Times

Photographs:
All photographs used in this book came from the Library of Congress Prints and Photographs Division Washington, D.C.

Often Quoted Index

This is an Index of the quotes made by the most often quoted people in this book. Each quote in this book has a number. The numbers below the names are the numbers of the quotes which were made by that individual. An exception to this quote Index methodology is John Brown. With John Brown there is included both the numbers of the quotes which he made, and the numbers of the quotes about him that were made by others.

This book will be offered as an e-book and as a printed book. With each of the 501 quotes assigned a number, it should be easy enough using this indexing method to locate quotes in both book formats.

Abraham Lincoln

1 2 3 4 5 10 11 14 15 17 22 35 36 37 38 40 41 42 43 44 53 61 79 80 84 95 98 100 113 116 127 129 136 149 160 161 162 165 166 167 168 171 172 173 174 175 185 202 204 206 241 248 249 253 254 256 288 293 297 328 329 331 338 342 345 352 367 368 369 370 378 369 370 378 380 386 401 424 427 444 446 447 450

Jefferson Davis

24 93 106 207 211 243 263 298 304

John Brown - Quotes By And About

10 28 184 188 190 191 192 193 194 195 196 198 199 200 201 202 203 204 205 256

Robert E. Lee

18 29 30 31 32 33 34 54 64 76 102 109 123 132 137 151 153 154 155 159 230 314 372 387 425 432 438 441 449

Thomas Jonathan "Stonewall" Jackson

57 59 60 62 63 65 130 139 310 377 418 436 470 471 496

Ulysses S. Grant

7 8 9 26 27 56 90 100 103 112 118 127 320 346 354 379 381

William Tecumseh Sherman

47 48 49 50 52 70 72 81 87 101 117 133 141 148 209 223 224 225
226 227 228 255 339 374 383 388 389 392 422 431 445 464 466 502

My Civil War Quotes and Notes Collection

As you learn more about the Civil War you will probably
find quotes and notes that you would like to remember.
Jot those quotes and notes down here in your own
Civil War Quotes and Notes Collection and turn this book
into 501+ Civil War Quotes and Notes.

My Civil War Quotes and Notes Collection

My Civil War Quotes and Notes Collection